COVENANT • BIBLE • STUDIES

The Household of God

Frank Ramirez

faithQuest® ♦ Brethren Press®

The Household of God
Covenant Bible Studies Series

Copyright © 2009 by *faithQuest*®. Published by Brethren Press®, 1451 Dundee Avenue, Elgin, IL 60120.

Library of Congress Cataloging-in-Publication Data

Ramirez, Frank, 1954-
    The household of God / Frank Ramirez.
        p. cm. — (Covenant Bible studies series)
    Summary: "Provides Bible study on 1 and 2 Timothy and Titus, known collectively as the pastoral letters, for use in a small group setting"—Provided by publisher.
    Includes bibliographical references (p.   ).
    ISBN 978-0-87178-126-0
 1. Bible. N.T. Pastoral Epistles—Textbooks. I. Title.

    BS2735.55.R36 2009
    227'.830071--dc22

                                                            2009013938

13 12 11 10 09   1 2 3 4 5

Manufactured in the United States of America

To Cally Suzanna Tamar Miller,
who at the age of five wrote such wonderful prayers
for the Household of God on September 11, 2001.

Contents

Foreword

The Covenant Bible Studies series provides *relational* Bible studies for people who want to study the Bible in small groups rather than alone.

Relational Bible study is marked by certain characteristics that differ from other types of Bible study. We are reminded that relational Bible study is anchored in covenantal history. God covenanted with people in Old Testament history, established a new covenant in Jesus Christ, and covenants with the church today. Thus, this Bible study is intended for small groups of people who can meet face-to-face on a regular basis and share frankly and covenant with one another in an intimate group.

Relational Bible study takes seriously a corporate faith. As each person contributes to study, prayer, and work, the group becomes the real body of Christ. Each one's contribution is needed and important. "For just as the body in one and has many members, and all the members of the body, though many, are one body, so it is with Christ. . . . Now you are the body of Christ and individually members of it" (1 Cor. 12:12, 27).

Relational Bible study helps both individuals and the group claim the promise of the Spirit and the working of the Spirit. As one person testified, "In our commitment to one another and in our sharing, something happened. . . . We were woven together in love by the Master Weaver. It is something that can happen only when two or three or seven are gathered in God's name, and we know the promise of God's presence in our lives."

In a small group environment, members aid one another in seeking to become

- biblically informed so they better understand the revelation of God;
- globally aware so they know themselves to be better connected with all of God's world;

• relationally sensitive to God, self, and others.

For people who choose to use this study in a small group, the following intentions will help create an atmosphere in which support will grow and faith will deepen.

1. As a small group of learners, we gather around God's word to discern its meaning for today.
2. The words, stories, and admonitions we find in scripture come alive for today, challenging and renewing us.
3. All people are learners and all are leaders.
4. Each person will contribute to the study, sharing the meaning found in the scripture and helping bring meaning to others.
5. We recognize each other's vulnerability as we share out of our own experience, and in sharing we learn to trust others and to be trustworthy.

The questions in the "Suggestions for Sharing and Prayer" section are intended for use in the hour preceding the Bible study to foster intimacy in the covenant group and to relate personal sharing to the Bible study topic, preparing one another to go out again in all directions to be in the world.

Welcome to this study. As you search the scriptures, may you also search yourself. May God's voice and guidance and the love and encouragement of brothers and sisters in Christ challenge you to live more fully the abundant life God promises.

Preface

Somewhere in my garage there's a box of papers from my years at Bethany Theological Seminary. I was blessed by an extraordinary faculty of individuals who were the tops in their field. I don't have to consult my notes from that time to recall what New Testament professor Dr. Graydon F. Snyder said once: that the only real heresy was taking anything out of scripture. We had to keep it all, and deal with it all.

However, there are times I'm tempted to ignore him when it comes to 1 and 2 Timothy, along with the letter to Titus, otherwise known as the pastoral letters. They include some of my favorite passages—and some that absolutely gall me.

I don't like the parts that accept slavery as a fact of life, or lay out a strictly patriarchal household structure. I don't. I've heard too many people quote verses from these letters to justify abuses—and even to abuse!

But there's no denying that there are also stirring passages in these books, some of which I quote all the time, at funerals, in sermons, and dedicatory events. Passages like the doxology from 1 Timothy 1:17, which includes the words, "immortal, invisible, the only God."

"He was revealed in flesh, vindicated in spirit, seen by angels, proclaimed among Gentiles, believed in throughout the world, taken up in glory" (1 Tim. 3:16).

"All scripture is inspired by God and is useful for teaching" (2 Tim. 3:16).

And finally, how can you perform a funeral without saying: "I have fought the good fight, I have finished the race, I have kept the faith" (2 Tim. 4:7)?

I hope you have seen the mistake I've made. Both the items that distress me and the verses I enjoy are taken out of context—the immediate context of the books involved, as well as the larger context of the society in which they are set.

Which leads me to the reason I am so excited about writing this study—I hope to place these Christian documents in the larger context of their situation and society. I think it all comes into focus with an exploration of the structure of the household in the first-century Roman Empire.

Instead of following the normal pattern of studying the letters chapter by chapter in consecutive order, I intend to divide them into readings that speak to the same issues.

I have titled this study, *The Household of God.* The first-century Roman household was an interesting and overblown structure that bore no resemblance to today's nuclear family, which is a rather recent development. This context helps us interpret the letters.

The household of God might have been modeled after Rome, but it was also transformed.

At one time I intended to call this study, *All Faith Is Local,* an allusion to the old saying from the late U.S. Congressman Tip O'Neill that all politics is local. The pastoral letters are largely concerned with local church and family issues rather than the broader issues of faith, though the latter are dealt with as well. However, these are precisely the issues that engage church, family, and church family, and that is why I think small groups will find this a fruitful study. May these scriptures prove "useful for teaching, for reproof, for correction, and for training in righteousness, so that everyone who belongs to God may be proficient, equipped for every good work (2 Tim. 3:16-17). Amen.

Frank Ramirez
Everett, Pennsylvania

1

Who, What, When, Where, and Why

Personal Preparation

1. Using a modern English translation, read these three New Testament letters in the following order: Titus, 1 Timothy, and 2 Timothy. Mark passages that strike you as interesting, alarming, intriguing, or memorable. Write a few sentences or paragraphs about your initial impressions of these letters.
2. Then look up the introductions to these letters in a Bible dictionary or commentary. What do your resources say about the author and purpose of these letters?
3. If you are the leader of the group, you might hunt photos of Colossae, Crete, and Rome, and prepare a computer slideshow presentation. Also prepare a map with these locations clearly marked.
4. Print out words and music for "Teresa's Prayer" by Joseph Helfrich from http://rockhay.tripod.com/worship/music/teresaprayer.htm.

Suggestions for Sharing and Prayer

1. Gather together in a comfortable setting. Begin by greeting one another. If this is the first time together for this group, make introductions. If group members are familiar with one another, take time to catch up on what has been happening since the last time you were together.
2. If a slideshow and map presentation has been prepared, take time to watch, share, and ask questions of each

other. There is also information about Colossae, Crete, and Rome in the "Understanding" section of this chapter.

3. In the ancient world, Bible reading was Bible listening. Probably only two to four percent of the population was literate as we know it, but they were intelligent and listened intently to scripture when it was read aloud in worship. This is how most people at that time encountered scripture. Though it will take up most of this first session of sharing and prayer, listen to the scriptures being read aloud. One person from the group might be the reader, but it would better if three or four share the experience. A leader should divide up the readings ahead of time.

4. Do not follow along in your own Bible. Let the word become flesh and dwell among you as the readers bring something of their own experience with God and life to the reading. The listening experience is ideally subject to different qualities of voice and personality.

5. Following the readings, take a moment to stand and stretch. Remain standing, if comfortable, and without referring to the written text, pray aloud in turn, basing your prayers on those portions of the scripture that were memorable for you.

6. Closing by singing "Teresa's Prayer" by Joseph Helfrich.

Understanding

Jim Hardenbrook, a pastor from Idaho and one-time chaplain for the state assembly, once mentioned that as a boy from the West he viewed the Bible through his own cultural lens.

When he first heard about Jesus delivering the Sermon on the Mount, he assumed that Jesus was mounted on a horse, speaking to his *compadres* who were on mounts of their own. There was nothing odd to him about this mental picture. How else would a group of *pardners* chew the fat if not on horses?

We all bring cultural assumptions to our reading of the Bible, but most of us aren't aware that we're doing so. When we think of New Testament churches we mentally put them in large structures built specifically for worship. We imagine that Paul wrote his letters by putting pen to papyrus. When we hear about an apostle addressing a family we're likely to picture mom, dad, and a couple of kids.

Then, when someone corrects us and tells us that the earliest Christians worshiped in house churches, we're likely to picture some friends meeting quietly in a living room for Bible study.

We assume folks in Bible times looked, thought, and acted pretty much like us, yet to understand what's really being said in these letters it's helpful to know something about their world. Though twenty-first-century America and first-century Rome are roughly the same size, crisscrossed by highways, and multicultural polyglots, the differences are far greater.

Getting All the Facts

In high school I learned the basics of journalism: who, what, when, where, and why. A fair, balanced story requires all of these.

Who? The author identifies himself as the apostle Paul. Some have suggested that the tone, vocabulary, subject matter, and voice in these letters differ from other Pauline letters. Yet they contain autobiographical details that seem authentic. Some suggest the differences are due to the fact that Paul was now older, that the churches were dealing with different issues, and that Paul might have dictated them to a different secretary.

As to the addressees, that would seem to be clear—Timothy and Titus were younger associates of the apostle, and their churches were also addressed. When we think of a church, we tend to think of a building. If not a cathedral, at least a structure designed and built for worship. However, a first-century house church included family members, slaves, servants, artisans, artists, and others, who shared public rooms, living quarters, areas where crafts were practiced, cooking facilities, and places to raise children.

What? These documents are letters, and they are addressed, as stated earlier, not just to individuals, but to their churches.

Personal letters in ancient times began with a greeting formula: a wish for the addressee's health and a short prayer. The main body of the ancient letter was usually concerned with maintaining contact, expressing feelings, providing information, or making requests.

The letters closed with another wish for health, usually translated as "farewell" or "good-bye." There were also salutations to and from friends or family, as well as another prayer. The end of the letter might include notification of a coming visit, a request for a return letter, or a reiteration of why the letter was written in the first place.

We who communicate instantly through cheap long distance and e-mail have little conception of what it would be like to communicate slowly. At least with Roman roads, mail in the empire moved much more reliably than it would have in the centuries between then and now.

When? These letters were written during the first Christian century. There are those who insist that these letters were written in the late first or early second century. I'm not convinced. The letters insist it is possible for the Christian to work within the larger society while respecting government. The letters assume one can live within the larger society. There are no references to either the persecution by the Emperor Nero during the 60s or the fall of Jerusalem in AD 71. But more on this discussion later.

Where? Paul wrote from Rome, the center of a far-reaching empire, and a polyglot of cultures, languages, religions, and races, with an astounding gulf between the very rich and nearly everyone else. He wrote to Christians living in Colossae, Crete, and Rome.

Paul had not yet visited Colossae in Asia Minor when he wrote two letters from prison, Colossians and Philemon. The church there was evidently founded by a Christian named Epaphras. Though at one time it had been a significant city known for its wool and located along a major highway, by the first Christian century Colossae had dwindled in importance, perhaps because of an earthquake.

The island of Crete was the home of the ancient Minoan civilization and its people were fiercely independent. Jews from Crete were among those who first heard the gospel preached by Peter after Pentecost, and some of these people probably formed the core of the island's Christian church. Paul left Titus in Crete to oversee the Christian faith there.

The city of Rome was preeminent in the Roman Empire, so we might expect the Christians at Rome to think they were at the center of the universe as well. However, there is no evidence to suggest that Rome or the leaders of the Roman church were considered superior to any others. Tradition to the contrary, there is no biblical evidence that the apostle Peter ever went there or was considered the leader of the Roman church. However, as the seat of empire, government officials saw a political threat in Christianity's claim that Jesus is Lord and, from the time of Nero, actively scapegoated and persecuted Christians.

Why? As mentioned a little earlier, in other letters the apostle was tending to the problems facing new churches with a new faith. Now the author is not establishing fellowships, but attempting to maintain them. Like any loving relationship, after the courtship and the craziness are over the long-term love begins, and that requires hard work. It is not easy to abide in love, not even God's love.

The writer is also concerned about the way the church appears to the outside world. Accusations against Christian house churches led to suspicion by the Roman authorities, who could be fairly tolerant about almost anything unless it threatened the foundations of society.

There are contradictions between these letters and earlier documents by the apostle Paul and other authors. Some attempt to smooth out these differences to present the Christian writings as a consistent whole. Others suggest that the New Testament is a dialogue about Jesus and what it means to be a disciple contested between differing viewpoints. According to this view, within the pages of the New Testament it is not always a matter of either/or; sometimes it's both/and.

In the New Testament, as in life, opposites rest side by side. The church was anxiously waiting for the imminent return of Jesus; the church was also setting up structures for long-term maintenance. Women were not allowed to take part in ministry; women were active in ministry. The early church was an egalitarian society that held all things in common; the early church established a clear chain of command and the beginnings of a hierarchy.

How to settle such contradictions? Context. Establishing the social context, which was group-oriented rather than individualistic as in our age, provides insight into the early church and helps establish applicability and relevance.

Discussion and Action

1. What cultural lens do you use when you read scripture? What is your economic, national, religious, ethnic, and racial background? How does that affect the way you hear and interpret scripture?

2. What theme or issue impressed you in your hearing of these letters? What themes seem antiquated or outdated? Describe your reactions to some of the things you heard.

3. If you were a first-century Christian hearing one of these letters for the first time, what do you think would have stuck in your head? Would this be something that pleased or distressed you? Explain. Would it matter if you were slave or free, male or female, rich or poor when you listened?

4. When you were a child, how did you picture Jesus? How did you picture the ancient church or the apostle Paul? In what ways has your viewpoint changed over the years? In what ways has your viewpoint remained the same?

5. In "Personal Preparation" you were asked to write out your reflections on the purpose of these letters. Read these sentences out loud. Compare and contrast your varying conclusions. Why do you think people experience the same document in similar and different ways? What do you think informed your hearing?

6. To what extent does considering that these letters are part of the Word of God affect the way you evaluate them? Are biblical documents to be evaluated differently than the way you would evaluate other documents from the ancient world or writings from the modern age? Explain.
7. What structures exist in your own fellowship and denomination? If there are both official and unofficial hierarchies, how did they originate? What, if any, parallels to these hierarchies do you hear in these letters?

2

The Paul of the Pastoral Letters
Titus 1:1-3; 1 Timothy 1:1;
2 Timothy 1:1, 8-12; 2:8-10; 3:10-13

Personal Preparation

1   Read the passages listed above aloud, a practice you will be encouraged to use for the entire study. Make notes about portions that intrigue you.

2. List five things you "know" about the apostle Paul. Bring these to "Sharing and Prayer" time. Now read a short biography of Paul on the Internet or in a study Bible. Find Tarsus, Cyprus, Damascus, and Jerusalem on a Bible map.

3. Name the civic connections that define you—clubs, professional organizations, sports teams, memberships, and other identities. Where do these different worlds intersect?

4. Is there a congregational history available for your church? If so, read it and bring it to the session. Try to write one paragraph about your denominational history to share with the group.

Suggestions for Sharing and Prayer

1. Greet one another with words of faith as you gather together. Share news of the past week, as well as your impressions of these passages and this chapter of the study.

2. Discuss what you've learned about the apostle Paul—both the things you "know" and what you discovered in your reading.

3. On a whiteboard or piece of newsprint, list all the civic connections you discovered about yourselves. Work them into larger networks to show how group members' lives intersect.

4. In the light of the biographies of Paul you researched, ask yourselves: Who is the Paul presented in these letters? What do we know of him, biographically? Is he a person you would like to have met? What do you think he was like?

5. Discuss the history of your local congregation or covenant group. How important or unimportant were individuals to the founding of these entities? How important is personality in the life of the church? Where do you fit in the history of your congregation and denomination?

6. Condense your life story into a two-minute biography. Tell each other your stories. Invite group members to add or edit your oral account. Name strengths about one another.

7. Lift up prayers for your denomination, congregation, and Christendom, as well as prayers for the preservation of your covenant group. Close by singing "The Church's One Foundation."

Understanding

As a writer and preacher at special events, I'm used to getting requests for a short biography. I generally include where I live, how long I've been married, the number of my children and grandchildren, and maybe something about my hobbies.

It would be nice if, at the end of one of Paul's letters, we were to read something like: *Saul/Paul, a native of Tarsus, was raised in Jerusalem and studied under the famed rabbi, Gamaliel. A widower, he is best known for his extensive travels throughout the Roman Empire in support of The Way and for his correspondence, which is treasured by all who receive it. These letters include . . . .*

Is that too much to ask? It sure would help. But in Paul's day the idea of autobiography as we know it simply did not exist.

It doesn't mean we know nothing about him. The Acts of the Apostles and his letters are filled with biographical detail. But these facts must be filtered through what we know of the purpose of the letters and Acts.

Any biography of Paul is speculative, based on references in scripture that are sometimes subject to more than one interpretation. Even so, here goes.

Paul: A Life
Paul was probably born between AD 5 and 10 in Tarsus in Cilicia near the southern coast of Asia Minor. His parents were Jews who held special status as citizens of Rome, perhaps for service they or their ancestors had performed for the Roman Empire. It was normal for Jews to have both a Hebrew and Greek name. He probably used both throughout his life. One often hears that after his conversion he dropped the name Saul and became Paul, but that is not what happens in Acts. He continues to use Saul after his conversion until he was in Cyprus, visiting with the proconsul Sergius Paulus, who shared the same name with him (Acts 13:4-12). After this, his work in the empire seemed to require the use of his Greek name, Paul.

Saul's family seems to have moved to Jerusalem when he was very young, where he was taught by Rabbi Gamaliel, who was considered one of the great Jewish teachers of the age (Acts 22:3).

At some point Paul was married. Greek verbs used in 2 Corinthians strongly suggest he was a widower, but there is no indication when or how his wife died, nor if he had children, and if so, who took care of them after his wife's death.

A zealot for Jewish orthodoxy, Saul freely admitted that he persecuted the new church of Jesus the Christ in Judea and Samaria, and though he did not participate in the stoning of Stephen, the first Christian martyr, he took care of the coats and consented to the death (Acts 7:54–8:3).

It's unclear when his conversion to Christianity took place. Where it happened is clearer—on the Damascus road (Acts 9:1-22). After his powerful encounter with Jesus, he was baptized and lived for a time in the region east of Damascus. He did not at first seek out any of the apostles or relatives of Jesus. For some time, Christians feared him, even after Barnabas vouched for him (Acts 9:26-27). Eventually Paul began to preach in Damascus, which got him into some trouble. Three years after his conversion he finally went to Jerusalem to meet with Peter and James, the brother of Jesus. Throughout his missionary journeys, he stood up to established leadership in the Jewish, Christian, and Gentile worlds, and as a result he suffered greatly.

Paul considered it his mission to extend the faith beyond the comfortable boundaries of those who shared his ethnic background. He described himself as an apostle, a trusted emissary of Jesus, for whom he suffered hardship. He disagreed with those believers who insisted that one needed to become an ethnic Jew in order to follow Jesus, despite the fact that he remained a practicing Jew all of his days.

Describing his personal sacrifices, Paul wrote:

Five times I have received from the Jews the forty lashes minus one. Three times I was beaten with rods. Once I received a stoning. Three times I was shipwrecked; for a night and a day I was adrift at sea; on frequent journeys, in danger from rivers, danger from bandits, danger from my own people, danger from Gentiles, danger in the city, danger in the wilderness, danger at sea, danger from false brothers and sisters; in toil and hardship, through many a sleepless night, hungry and thirsty, often without food, cold and naked. (2 Cor. 11:24-27)

Paul spoke in ecstatic utterances, although he insisted the phenomenon wasn't as important as clear preaching. He also suffered from a "thorn in the flesh," which some suggest may have been depression, schizophrenia, or epileptic seizures, but which I think may have been an eye problem for which the Celts (in Galatia) may have provided some treatment (2 Cor. 12:7-10; Gal. 4:13-15).

His greatest moment may have taken place at the great Council of Jerusalem around AD 49, when Jewish Christian leaders agreed that Gentile converts could retain their ethnic identities, though they must of course renounce idolatry and immoral behavior (Acts 15).

The New Testament chronicles several imprisonments. Acts ends with Paul in house arrest in Rome somewhere around AD 60-62 on a false charge that he was spreading sedition by espousing Jewish messianism. It seems likely that he was exonerated of these charges, but there is a strong tradition he was imprisoned once more in Rome a few years later under much harsher circumstances when Emperor Nero went on a rampage against Christians. According to this tradition he was beheaded, perhaps sometime between AD 64 and 67.

So, Who Wrote What?

Despite the fact that the two letters to Timothy and the letter to Titus claim to be from Paul, there are those who suggest someone else wrote them. The reasons include a difference in vocabulary, tone, and topic. For instance, Paul normally debates his unseen opponents, but in these letters he dismisses them out of hand.

And instead of focusing on theological arguments about the nature of Jesus, salvation, the relationship of the law to grace, and controversies about Gentile and Jewish practices, the author of these letters is more concerned with relationships within the household and church hierarchy. At the most, some would admit that a few biographical passages from authentic letters have been woven into false material to lend it some authenticity.

There is much to be said for these arguments. But as a writer myself, I know that one's writing can look a great deal different depending on age, purpose, and the slow change of years. Consider Shakespeare. It's hard to imagine that the same person wrote the incredibly gory *Titus Andronicus*, the witty and clever

Love's Labor's Lost, with its almost impenetrable net of inside jokes, the extraordinarily complex *Hamlet,* with its many layers of meaning, and the valedictory resurrection play *The Tempest,* where revenge is averted and all is made well.

But it all makes perfect sense when you realize that *Titus* was written to compete with the popular bloodfests of Christopher Marlowe, *Love's Labor's Lost* was written to please a small coterie when the public theaters were closed for the plague, *Hamlet* was written to fill a brand new stage once the author himself became an owner and shareholder in the enterprise, and *The Tempest* may have been written when the author had retired in the country, away from the hurly burly of London.

Even in the authenticated letters of Paul there is a difference between his concern about the imminent return of Jesus in early letters, such as the two to Thessalonica, and such classic letters as Romans and 1 Corinthians, where it is not a major issue.

The difference in vocabulary and tone may come simply from the fact that Paul was using a different scribe. He did not write these letters himself. He dictated them, and it is thought that some scribes took more liberties during dictation than others.

In *Stewards, Prophets, Keepers of the Word: Leadership in the Early Church,* Ritva H. Williams suggests that in the early church Stewards took care of the physical needs of the faithful, Prophets with their altered states of consciousness kept the door open between heaven and earth, while Keepers of the Word interpreted scripture to preserve tradition and collective memory as a way of providing continuity and supporting change. Each had their function. And she demonstrates in her book how the apostle Paul fulfilled all three roles at different times in his ministry.

Regardless of what you may choose to believe, these letters were considered valuable enough to be preserved and protected by the community of faith. For the purpose of this study the author will be referred to as Paul.

Discussion and Action

1. How have you changed over the years? Would people from your past recognize you now in terms of beliefs,

practices, and preferences? Do you write the same, enjoy the same foods, belong to the same political party as when you were younger?

2. Are our congregations in places where everyone is welcome regardless of background, or do we intentionally or subconsciously enforce a certain conformity? Explain your response. If there are differences of opinion, explore how people can perceive the same congregation in different ways.

3. How do we identify ourselves as individuals, small groups, and congregations to our communities and the world? Are our mission and ministries aimed at including all?

4. What titles do we claim for ourselves? What memberships in civic, professional, recreational, and religious groups do you have? Look back at the social networks you mapped in "Sharing and Prayer" time. Where are the intersections among your networks? How do these intersections affect your life of faith?

5. What is your impression of Paul? Would Paul be someone you would enjoy meeting? Why, or why not? What don't you know about the apostle Paul that intrigues you?

6. How important is biography in the life of your church? How well do people know each other's stories? What difference, if any, do relationships and history with your congregation make in the way people are treated? How has this changed over the years?

3

Timothy and Titus,
You've Got Mail
*Titus 1:4-9; 1 Timothy 1:2; 3:1-13;
2 Timothy 1:2-7; 3:14-17*

Personal Preparation

1. Read these passages aloud, noting verses that intrigue, alarm, inspire, or interest you. Listen to your own voice as you read. What difference does it make in hearing the text?
2. Find an important personal letter or e-mail you wrote or received that you feel comfortable sharing with the group.
3. What qualifications are required for leadership in your congregation? For church membership? For membership in this covenant group? For your job position or situation?
4. Think about the different officers who administrate your church. Which hold spiritual offices? Which are administrative? Is there a clear difference between the categories? How do you define these terms?

Suggestions for Sharing and Prayer

1. Greet each other with a short prayer for health. Then share the letters or e-mails you brought. Discuss what sorts of things you would or would not include in different forms of communication. How personal is your personal correspondence? What place do letters have in

our society, and how has that changed over time, in your opinion?
2. Read today's passages aloud. Listen closely if you are not reading.
3. Reflect together on the structure of your church and denomination. Discuss whether your church structures help or impede honest communication. How willingly and openly do people share? What sorts of information get passed along? How much is written down?
4. This session discusses some of the structure of first-century house churches. How do any of your current positions correspond, or contradict, with the structures of the early church? How does this aid or impede your ministries?
5. Hang up newsprint and take markers in hand. Work together on a letter to God. What sorts of things are you curious about, or what questions do you want answers to? What tone do you think would be the most appropriate? After the letter is written, take time to pray your letter together.
6. Gather in a circle. Share sentence prayers for each other that lift up some of what you have learned about each other in this session. Move on to extended prayers for leaders at all levels of your faith lives. Close by singing "What Is This Place" or another hymn about the nature of the church.

Understanding

English is the official language of the Central American nation of Belize. Though the dialect is different from the English of the United States, it follows its own rules and is perfectly correct. The slogan of Quality Chicken, run by Belizean Mennonites, is "Dis da fu we chicken," which means "This (is) our chicken." Same language, really. But a different dialect.

A little over a century ago, students of ancient Greek were warned when introduced to the New Testament writings that the apostles were uneducated men who wrote poorly. Then papyrus documents were discovered in the Egyptian desert: receipts, letters, invitations, official notices—all written in the same style as the New Testament.

Scholars realized that "business" Greek was different from "literary" Greek. Like the English of Belize, it followed its own rules and was perfectly correct. This business Greek was the second language of the Roman Empire. It was not fancy, but it got the job done.

The New Testament was written in business, not literary, Greek. Far from being primitive, the New Testament authors drew from words rich in practical meaning as they told our Christian story. Their words are *life* words, not theological words. Debts are debts. Baptize is a word used for washing dishes or clothes, and means dunking all the way under water. Pastors are shepherds. Deacons are waiters. Bishops are not ecclesiastical officers with tall hats; the word refers to a slave who acts as overseer or straw boss.

Dis da fu we church.

Backstory

Judging from internal evidence, Paul wrote the letter to Titus, who was in Crete, and the first letter to Timothy, who was in Ephesus at the time, while traveling on the road from Macedonia and Nicopolis in northwest Greece. The second letter to Timothy is written from prison in Rome.

Timothy was a well-known associate of Paul. Paul referred to him as his child because he had been involved in his conversion (Acts 16:1-3; Phil. 2:22). He is listed as a co-writer of more than one of Paul's letters. He had been Paul's envoy to Thessalonica (1 Thess. 3:2, 6) and Corinth (1 Cor. 4:17; 16:10), and he is presented in these letters as representing Paul in Ephesus. He may have had a Gentile father and a Jewish mother. As was typical in the Roman Empire, his mother was the one who was responsible for his upbringing and education.

Like Timothy, Titus was converted at some point in Paul's ministry, and is referred to as "his child." He was also something of a trophy that Paul displayed to the Gentile world, bragging that Titus, though Gentile in birth, was not required to be circumcised when he joined the faith (Gal. 2:1-3). Paul trusted him, and appointed him to lead the church in Crete, where he was also assigned the task of collecting a love offering to help the poor Christians of Jerusalem.

Stewards, Prophets, and Keepers of the Word

In the pastoral letters, Paul is also interested in church structure, something that doesn't engage him much in the other letters. Some see an interest in ecclesiastical offices as proof that they were written after Paul's death. But it is dangerous to interpret words in the light of our own experience.

The books listed as resources in the bibliography are very helpful in describing the first-century church. I'm especially intrigued by *Stewards, Prophets, Keepers of the Word: Leadership in the Early Church* by Ritva H. Williams. It's an excellent book about house churches in the first Christian century. It begins by describing what households were actually like, then examines the evidence for Stewards (slaves who ran the household), Prophets (who revealed the Spirit through altered states of consciousness), and Keepers of the Word (who preserve the received tradition). All three were necessary for the early church, and the implication is that we still need servant— or slave—leadership, as well as space for prophets and keepers of the word. The evidence is strong from the New Testament and early Christian literature that this was the case. Certainly in every denomination's history there is tension between Prophets, who make us especially uncomfortable with their saint-like example and to-the-point words, and Stewards, who include our capable administrators, as well as Keepers of the Word.

The word translated as bishop is overseer, or straw boss. Bishops, as mentioned earlier, are not so much a part of set-apart ministry as they are practical overseers of the work of the church, fellow slaves of Jesus Christ. This is not a person who stands on higher spiritual ground and is able to perform offices that no one else is allowed, or who pronounces theological truths from on high. This is a person who is at ground level, helping to organize for the benefit of all. Personal letters from the ancient world make it clear that these overseers were just as concerned with the financial well-being of Christians as their spiritual health. Bishops probably looked after the economic structure of the believers more than their faith relationships.

This practice continued long after Paul's time, as seen in a personal letter written between AD 264-282 by a businessman who tells his associate that the money from the sale of cloth and wheat be delivered to the care of Maximus, the bishop of Alexandria, or "let it be entrusted, giving it to Theonas," who would one day succeed him in that office. The letter writer notes, "We have profited by his dealings . . . with him" (author's translation from the Greek).

This financial oversight was necessary because converts to Christianity were often cut off from relatives because of their faith choices. They seem to have formed families who practiced trades or crafts together, and were allied in an economy. It's worth remembering that the Greek word for house, *oikos*, from which our modern world economy is derived, is also the source of the words ecumenical and fellowship. Household, economy, and our fellowship with believers on both a local and larger situation come from the same word.

The term for deacons comes from a word that means table waiter, and describes the practical way in which they are to serve, not rule over, others. This designation signifies that they take care of the practical needs of the believers, especially with regards to the common meals. Paul uses the term steward to identify the slave who runs the household. Servant leadership, slave leadership, may be an uncomfortable concept for those who think of leadership in terms of power. The first-century church did not.

It seems to me that elders are just what they sound like— older folks revered for their wisdom. And indeed, "family" ties may be stronger bonds than those formed by laity with official leaders of the church.

That's why it's worth noting that the most significant office may be that of mom and grandma! Paul commends the work of Timothy's mother and grandmother, Lois and Eunice (2 Tim. 1:5). In *A Woman's Place: House Churches in Earliest Christianity*, Carolyn Osiek and Margaret Y. MacDonald emphasize that "the Pastoral Epistles offer specific evidence of women being involved in the Christian socialization of children" (239). They say that this influence continued even after the children grew older and attained adulthood. Women ran the household, which included the raising of children. The relationship between mother and son seems to have been both formative and lasting.

Discussion and Action

1. With what sorts of church hierarchies are you familiar? Are these hierarchies of service or of rule? Are there unofficial and unwritten rules that everyone knows about and no one wants to break? Explain your responses.

2. Do you write letters? If so, what do you include in your letters? What things would you never reveal? Do you write e-mails? How do e-mails function differently for you? What sort of information do you include in e-mails? Have you ever written anything in a letter or e-mail that you regret? Share it with the group if you feel comfortable doing so.

3. What sorts of titles are used in your church? Which are most important in name? Which are more important in reality?

4. The chapter talks about the tension between Prophets, Stewards, and Keepers of the Word in the first-century church. Who, if anyone, in your church would fit under those titles? Which of these groups may be under-represented in your congregational life? Which may be over-represented? Why might this be so? Which do you fit in?

5. Think about the different officers who help your church function. Which are spiritual offices? Which are administrative? Is there a clear difference between the categories? How do you define these terms?

6. Consider some of the offices of house churches that are described in the session. What, if anything, in your life corresponds to the ancient household? Discuss what role the modern church should play in the economic

relationship between church members. Are our times more or less individualistic than the first-century Roman Empire? Give examples to explain your response.

4

The Household of God vs. the Household of Rome
Titus 2:1-10; 1 Timothy 2:8-15;
5:1–6:5; 2 Timothy 2:19-21

Personal Preparation

1. Read the passages out loud. Listen to the way the words sound. What is the place of men and women in your congregation, both stated and actual? In your household?
2. Search the Internet for information on Craig Kielburg and his crusade to rescue children around the world from slavery and abuse. Find out if your denomination or congregation works on similar issues. Bring information to the session.
3. Make a listing of "ordinary" things around your house. What is the significance and value of these items? Think of the origin and story of these items.
4. Read the Mark Twain quote in this session (p. 27). What injustices are you aware of that society in general, and perhaps you in particular, are willing to tolerate or even justify?

Suggestions for Sharing and Prayer

1. Greet each other. Gather for a time of silent prayer. Take time to listen to yourself, to others in the silence, and to God.

2. Read today's scriptures out loud. Discuss your initial
   reactions to these texts. How do you feel about these
   attitudes and their presence in scripture? How does your
   church approach matters of hierarchy and relationship?
   How do you interpret or evaluate scriptures such as
   these?
3. Now read the Mark Twain quote from the session aloud.
   Consider injustices in your own society or community.
   What justifications do we make for these? How intoler-
   able must things be before you and others are willing to
   act?
4. Discuss the place of women and men in your church,
   both stated and actual. How do your practices match up
   with society's norms? In what ways does your church
   present an exception to the world's norms?
5. Discuss the information group members found on Craig
   Kielburg or other programs aimed at ending modern-day
   slavery. How might individual members or your group
   get more involved in matters of justice?
6. Reflect on 2 Timothy 2:19-21. Then look at your lists of
   ordinary things. Which items are found on the lists of
   many group members? Which are unique to one or two
   households? Say prayers of dedication for these ordinary things, offering them up to God and for God's use.
7. Close with prayers for God's presence and action in
   your lives. Begin by offering thanks for the gift of ordinary things and for extraordinary people.

Understanding

Long ago on our tenth anniversary, Jennie and I spent a few days
in Santa Barbara, California. In addition to walking along the
beach, shopping in all the used bookstores, and eating at new
restaurants, we went to a beautiful, old-style movie theater that
had been lovingly preserved. Among many historic events, it
had hosted the West Coast premiere of *Gone with the Wind*.

I mention that movie because I believe the image of slavery
that existed for a couple of generations of white Americans was

based not so much on actual history as it was on images from this particular book and movie. As a result, the brutal legacy of casual rape, torture, and abuse was replaced with images of a fairly benevolent partnership that seemed to benefit everyone. Not much to do with reality.

Mark Twain, writing in his autobiography (volume one, p. 123), noted:

> As I have said, we lived in a slaveholding community; indeed, when slavery perished my mother had been in daily touch with it for sixty years. Yet, kind-hearted and compassionate as she was, I think she was not conscious that slavery was a bald, grotesque, and unwarrantable usurpation. She had never heard it assailed in any pulpit, but had heard it defended and sanctified in a thousand; her ears were familiar with Bible texts that approved it, but if there were any that disapproved it they had not been quoted by her pastors; as far as her experience went, the wise and the good and the holy were unanimous in the conviction that slavery was right, righteous, sacred, the peculiar pet of the Deity, and a condition which the slave himself ought to be daily and nightly thankful for. Manifestly, training and association can accomplish strange miracles.

This session's passages from the pastoral letters probably demonstrate most clearly the contrast between the household of Rome and the household of God. Both utilize the same basic materials. What then is the difference? The household of God is a transformed society, then and now.

The social assumptions of the Roman household—the presence of slaves, subservient wives, autocratic husbands and masters—seem to be at odds with our egalitarian society. And where would our modern church be without women to serve as pastors, board chairs, chairs of committees and commissions, Sunday school teachers, worship leaders, and all other aspects of Christian ministry?

We forget sometimes that we live in a society where we can work for change. The church can be at the forefront of that change, as demonstrated by Martin Luther King, Jr. and the non-violent struggles against racism and for civil rights. During the first century, Christians such as Paul could not change the fundamental platform of their society. But they could change hearts.

Who's the Boss?

The Roman household was a complex economy that included hierarchies of relatives: children, grandchildren, parents, grandparents, cousins, aunts, uncles, various wards, as well as servants and slaves, and attendant trade and craft experts. Everyone—the large extended family, slaves, artisans—lived together. The household had public areas where business could be transacted, work areas where the family craft took place, along with family areas where women held sway.

Slavery was an ugly fact of life in the ancient world, but unlike American slavery, slavery in the ancient world was an economic and not a race-based proposition. Therefore, it was not assumed that some races were inferior and destined for slavery. Slaves might have fallen to their position because they could not keep up with their debts. They might have been born into slavery. They might have been captured in war.

Because slaves were not considered an inferior sub-race, slaves had great responsibility for running all aspects of a business. Indeed, it was considered beneath an honorable citizen to be concerned with profit making—that was left to the slaves. Even so, slavery was still horrible. Slaves were subject to the cruelty or kindness of their master.

The household was headed by a *paterfamilias*, an autocratic male who was the absolute authority in all things. He arranged—and unarranged—marriages, settled all disputes, and held the power of life and death over everyone. The *paterfamilias* also had the right to use any member of the house physically or sexually as he chose.

Though a male was the head of a family, the wife was in charge of household matters, including the management of finances and family. She was the administrator. And since churches met in houses, and indeed might have been linked with households, many historians are coming to realize that women must have run the first-century churches as well. Artwork shows women administering the Love Feast and Eucharist meals. It is apparent from all that was written, including documents such as the first-century *Didache*, that unlike society at large, everyone—women, men, slaves, free—ate at the same table. It is also clear from New Testament documents, including letters of Paul, that women such as Lydia, Mary the mother of Mark (who owned the upper room), Priscilla, the apostle Junia, and others were leaders of house churches. While some Pauline documents acknowledge women in leadership positions, there are others that seem to silence them.

But Carolyn Osiek and Margaret Y. MacDonald makes it clear in their book, *A Woman's Place*, that "to step into a Christian house church was to step into women's world" (163).

Why does Paul contradict himself on the subject of women and ministry? I think what is really happening in these passages is that Paul is telling the church that "until folks get to know us we need to present as good a face to the world as possible." In other words, do not give unnecessary offense. At least, superficially. Once people get to know us they're going to realize we're as flawed as they are, but by that time we'll be in love with each other as people of Jesus Christ, so it won't matter.

Neither the church of the first century nor the church of the twenty-first century is in danger of appearing the least bit perfect—at least until we're perfected by Jesus Christ.

Paul and the first-century Christians were attempting to transform the household of Rome into a household of God in which there was accountability in both directions, recognition of the worth of all people, and the acknowledgement that Jesus—not any god-emperor—is the overarching Lord over all.

More importantly, Paul was establishing that the *paterfamilias* was not the be-all and end-all as in Roman society. There was a greater Lord and Master, Jesus Christ, who took priority over all other commitments. If society could not be reformed, then the church should be transformed.

In the end, everyone and everything in the household—master and slave, as well as utensils made of gold and wood—must be dedicated to the true "owner of the house, ready for every good work" (2 Tim. 2:21).

Discussion and Action

1. Discuss your initial reactions to these texts. How do you feel about these attitudes and their presence in scripture? How does your church approach matters of hierarchy and relationship? How do you interpret or evaluate scriptures such as these?

2. How does your family, past and present, work? Who is accountable to whom? What are the responsibilities? How are decisions made?

3. Can you think of an example of transformation, when individuals in a relationship became more accountable and responsible towards each other? Share these stories with one another, noting what led to the transformation and specific changes that resulted.

4. How have these texts appeared in sermons you have heard over the years? Were these sermons you enjoyed, questioned, rejected? What would you like to hear about these texts from the pulpit?

5. How important is the appearance we give as the church to the outside world? To what extent should we be accepted for who we are? How crucial is a relationship in accepting each other as we are?

6. Compare and contrast the family systems you have experienced with the Roman household. How are your systems informed by scripture? How is a living relationship with God part of your household structure? Use examples from your household to explain your responses.

7. It is easy to dismiss slavery as an evil from the past, but it is alive in our modern world. Yet most people manage to blind themselves towards its presence abroad, and even near at hand in the form of wage slaves and sweat shops. How can your group educate itself about the evils of slavery in the modern world? What can you do to combat slavery?

5

Render unto Caesar:
Obligations to Society
Titus 3:1-2; 1 Timothy 2:1-7; 2 Timothy 2:8-10

Personal Preparation

1. Read today's passages out loud to yourself. Note your initial responses to these texts.
2. There is a tendency for American Christians to confuse inconvenience with persecution. What do you know about the truly persecuted church? Use an Internet search engine to discover where Christians are actively being persecuted today.
3. Think about times, such as after September 11, 2001, when you may have viewed other religious groups with suspicion and believed rumors that were told about them to be true. Who came forward as an advocate for such groups? You? Your church? No one?
4. Try to find one false rumor and one true fact about another faith. Bring these with you to the session.

Suggestions for Sharing and Prayer

1. Greet one another with the sign of peace. One person says, "The peace of the blessed Lord be yours," and the other responds, "We share that same peace."
2. In countries like the U.S., people sometimes believe they are being persecuted because of imagined restrictions or supposed removal of religious symbols. Often

these turn out to be false rumors. Some of these false rumors include reports that Congress is removing religious programming from the airwaves, fears that the new dollar coins won't display the words, "In God We Trust," and so on. Come up with a list of other such false rumors you've heard recently. How do you respond when you hear such rumors?

3. When have you helped to spread rumors about others? When have you stood up for others? How much of your shared faith consists of conformity to the world? Share to the extent that you are able stories of compliance and timidity in the face of challenges to our faith. Offer up prayers of confession.

4. Now consider what you have learned about the persecuted church. Share the stories that you garnered from "Personal Preparation" time. Offer prayers for the persecuted church, for those in prison for their faith, for those suffering torture, loss of property, family, and even life itself.

5. Read today's passages out loud. Consider in silence your obligations to society and your obligations to Jesus. Conclude with spoken prayers for wisdom and discernment in making difficult choices.

Understanding

Into the twentieth century, German was spoken in many American cities. Cincinnati, Ohio, for instance, was a city where German predominated. German flags, German culture, and German festivals were commonplace.

That all changed with the entry of the United States into the European war. Fear reigned. Suddenly all Germans were portrayed as the enemy of humankind. Persecution and changing public attitudes led to the loss of German culture. People who criticized the government were arrested. Churches suddenly sprouted American flags in their sanctuaries to prove their patriotism. Only recently a group of German Americans who were arrested, tried, and imprisoned in North Dakota for the crime of expressing their opinion of the president were pardoned. Posthumously, of course.

It is one thing to look back and shake our heads at the excesses of another generation. But we need only remember the hysteria that followed the 9/11 attacks to realize that when people are afraid both dissent and difference are seen as treasonous, and churches fall over each other to line up behind any breach of civil rights that the government proposes.

This is the light in which we must look at these scriptures from Titus and Timothy, which are sometimes quoted along with Romans 13:1-7 as proof that we must always obey the government. The *Pax Romana*, Peace of Rome, had eliminated many wars between little rival kingdoms. The uniformity of Roman law insured justice on a scale previously unknown. As a citizen both of the Jewish and the Roman worlds, Paul took full advantage of Roman roads, Roman privileges, and Roman culture. Actually, he lived in at least three worlds: the Roman Empire, along with the Jewish societies of both Palestinian Jerusalem and the Diaspora.

Paul recognizes that all Christians live in a larger world, and says that we are not to retreat from it. Rather, we are "to be subject to rulers and authorities." This provides an opportunity for good works not simply for those in the community of faith, but for everyone (Titus 3:1-2). We are to pray for all rulers in the hope that we may live peaceably in society—especially because, as we are reminded by Paul, Jesus "gave himself a ransom for all," and that is why Paul has chosen to be an apostle to the Gentiles (1 Tim. 2:1-7).

Chains, Chains, Chains

Even so, in the final passage it is apparent that Paul has been imprisoned for his faith. There comes a point when Christians must part ways with the larger culture: "Remember Jesus Christ, raised from the dead, a descendant of David—that is my gospel, for which I suffer hardship, even to the point of being chained like a criminal. But the word of God is not chained. Therefore I endure everything for the sake of the elect, so that they may also obtain the salvation that is in Christ Jesus, with eternal glory" (2 Tim. 2:8-10).

The word of God is not chained, but Paul is. He ran afoul of the governing authorities when, after Rome was burned, Emperor Nero decided to scapegoat Christians and actively persecuted them. In those days it was easy to detect who was a Christian and who was not. Everyone in the Roman Empire was required to obtain a *libelli,* an official document that proved she or he had made an offering, perhaps only a pinch of spice thrown into the fire, to the emperor as a god. It's not clear if anyone believed for a moment the absurdity that any emperor was divine, but the legislation did not seek to control what people thought, only what they did.

Sometime in the second century, an anonymous Christian composed a letter to an official named Diognetus defending believers as good citizens. The letter countered rumors that Christians participated in strange and unnatural practices by arguing that Christians are noncomformists who challenge the world's standards yet do their best to be good neighbors:

> For Christians don't come from other countries, speak a different language, or act differently. They don't have their own economies, or dialect, nor do they have bizarre lifestyles. . . .
> They live according to chance in both Greek speaking and foreign cities, and dress the same, eat the same foods, act the same in all the rest of life's ways—except that they also paradoxically differently because of their citizenship. They live in the same countries, but they are foreigners. They take part in the political life of their land, but they endure the hardships of aliens. . . . They live on the earth but they are citizens of heaven. . . . They are put to death, but they are brought to life. They are made poor, but they make many rich. . . . People curse them but they bless in return. They honor those who insult them. . . . Simply put, Christians are to the world what the soul is to the body. (author's translation from the Greek)

The author then lists several contemporary customs, such as disposing of unwanted children or sharing spouses, which

Christians do not take part in, and adds that "they are poor, yet they make many rich; they are in need of everything, yet they abound in everything."

An Undeserved Reputation

Nevertheless, despite the desire of Christians to find their place in the larger society, they were labeled a "mischievous superstition" by the Roman historian Tacitas. Fellow historian Suetonius claimed they were a radical cult that sought to rule the world.

The Roman governor Pliny the Younger wrote to the Emperor Trajan around the year AD 115 to find out what limits he should set when hunting out Christians. He wrote that as far as he could tell this group seemed fairly harmless, and that they rose before dawn to share a meal and sing to Christ as to a god.

Pliny seems to be describing a household church like those to which Paul wrote. This church included two slave women whom Pliny described as deacons. He tortured them to discover what he could, but found nothing damning beyond the fact that they would not worship the Emperor as a god. That was the limit of their cooperation with the society.

During the Civil War, Dunkers (or Brethren), along with Mennonites and Quakers, suffered on both sides of the Mason-Dixon Line because they refused to take up arms. Things were much worse for those in the South than in the North. P. R. Wrightsman of Limestone, Tennessee, wrote after the war about an incident that took place in the summer of 1863:

> Southern soldiers . . . came from time to time for three years and took my crops and horses. . . . Their language and manner impressed me that they came with intent to kill me. . . . I just stepped inside the stable, stood with my hands upwards, and prayed to my heavenly Father, saying, "Dear Father, save me from these men. Have mercy upon them, and turn them from their evil course, and save thy servant."
>
> I never exercised stronger faith in prayer than at that time. It seemed as if I was speaking face to face with my blessed Lord. When I stepped out to the soldiers I felt that God had answered my prayer, for I could see the Satanic

look going down out of their faces like the shadow of a cloud before the bright sunlight.

The soldiers then said to me, "Mr. Wrightsman, can we get some bread?"

"O yes," said I, "we are commanded to feed the hungry." I went at once to the kitchen and requested my sisters to cut off a large slice of bread, and butter it for each of them. They did so and I took it out into the yard and handed a slice to each. They thanked me for the bread, bowed their heads, mounted their horses and rode away, taking my last horse with them, however. Feeling sure the Lord had saved my life, I felt happy, thanked God and took courage. (*The Olive Branch*)

Discussion and Action

1. When it comes to living in our society, what are your limits? How far will you cooperate with the government? Where do you draw the line? How has that line shifted over time and with circumstances? How do you determine the limits of your cooperation with government and society?

2. Some house churches and prayer groups eventually take on form and organization, and become more like structured churches. What does this say about them? Might it mean they have less faith—or perhaps that they have more endurance? Discuss your thoughts about this.

3. In what areas of the world is true persecution taking place today? Share what you found from your search in "Personal Preparation" time. How can Christians work to prevent persecution in our own society? How can we help those who live in other countries? What one action could your group take?

4. Paul says that though he might be in prison "the word of God is not chained." Does the gospel wear chains in your church? If so, what sorts of chains have you put on the gospel? For example, does the gospel wear chains in your church to prevent giving offense to others?

5. To what organizations do you belong? How have these organizations changed over time? Have they gained more structure over time, or become less structured? Discuss your views on whether long-term identity inevitably leads to an increasing structure.

6. A Christian wrote to Diognetes to defend Christianity from the charge that it was dangerous. How do you defend your faith when others claim you are not patriotic enough? As a group, try to come up with a unified statement in defense of your faith.

6

Works and Faith
Titus 3:3-8; 1 Timothy 1:8-11; 6:17-21;
2 Timothy 2:1-7

Personal Preparation

1. Read today's passages out loud. Which focus on the need for correct belief? Which emphasize correct action?

2. Research the terms "faith" and "works" in a Bible dictionary. Also, it may help to read Paul's letter to the Galatians and the letter of James.

3. Reflect on the value of things you've earned versus the value of things you've been given. Which mean more to you?

4. "Trial: Faith vs. Works" is one of the "Sharing and Prayer" suggestions. If you are the group leader and plan to use this simulation, contact group members and assign them to one of the sides. Members defending faith should study Galatians; members defending works should study the book of James.

Suggestions for Sharing and Prayer

1. Greet one another with the words, "The peace of the Lord be with you." Respond with, "And also with you." Take time to catch up on what has gone on in people's lives since the last time you met.

2. Do the simulation, "Trial: Faith vs. Works" (see page 73). If the group leader has not already done so, divide

into two groups. One group is headed by "Paul" and the other is led by "James" (don't let gender decide who you choose to play these parts). You are at the Council of Jerusalem in AD 49. There has been much miscommunication. The purpose of the tribunal is to decide the nature and character of the Christian faith. Follow the instructions to prepare for, participate in, and debrief the simulation.

3. Following the simulation, come together in prayer for the unity of all believers. You might pray Psalm 117 aloud, first reading individually and then as a group. Close with silent prayer.

Understanding

I'm more of an NBA than a NASCAR kind of guy. But I understand that some people's passion in following a driver can be the same as mine for the Los Angeles Lakers.

Many NASCAR fans where I live decorate their cars with the numbers of their favorite drivers. One car that intrigues me features the number of a driver who has died. He was by all accounts something of a rough and tumble character, yet his number often sports wings and a halo to show that he has now reached his heavenly reward.

It's fine with me if he's in paradise. However, that particular individual was not famous for his evangelical fervor but for driving aggressively, and not in a saint-like manner. But he won, and his fans liked that. What this tells me is that most Christians, despite all the talk about salvation by grace, deep down think it's not what you say, but what you do that matters.

Saved by Grace?

Christians believe we are saved by the grace of God and not by our works. The writings of the apostle Paul are the primary source of this belief. Jesus is no help at all. Jesus himself doesn't seem to care much about faith in Jesus. The Sermon on the Mount, for instance, seems very works oriented. In Matthew 25:31-46, Jesus describes an end-time judgment based totally on good works. In this passage he doesn't ask people if they have faith in him. He asks if they have served him by giving food to the hungry, drink to the thirsty, clothes to the naked, and by visiting the sick and those in prison. I do not recall a single verse in which he says, of himself, proclaim my name and be saved.

But there's a biblical basis to this grace thing as well. Paul seems to have been reacting to a belief that obedience to the law of God and correct religious observance, regardless of what was in one's heart, mattered more than justice and mercy. The prophets railed against this attitude for centuries, and Jesus called people back to justice and jubilee as well. Paul wants the people to know that it is not their obedience to an arbitrary understanding of God's standards that matters, but recognition that God has found us and saved us. This is grace, a gift.

Still, this belief that we are saved by grace can lead some people to totally ignore what it means to be a believer. For some, this has led to "once saved, always saved," in which believers state their belief in Jesus Christ as Lord and then sit on the sidelines, secure of their seat in heaven.

The writings of Paul don't support this "fire insurance" view of faith. One of Paul's greatest acts was organizing the collection for the poor Christians of Jerusalem among churches throughout the empire. He was arrested in the temple in Jerusalem while performing a good work for the benefit of those who had taken a Nazarite vow. That certainly supports the statement, "The saying is sure: . . . those who have come to believe in God . . . [should] devote themselves to good works" (Titus 3:8).

Though spontaneity in good works is important, Paul suggests that it wouldn't hurt to be prepared. In 2 Timothy 2:1-7, Paul uses the images of athletic and military training as well as the preparations for agriculture to serve as models for those who do good works. Works proceed from faith, and are a sign that a person is spiritually healthy.

Moreover, he scolds the rich (as did Jesus), reminding them not "to set their hopes on the uncertainty of riches, but rather on God who richly provides us with everything for our enjoyment."

Then he describes the importance of a life of works, saying, "They are to do good, to be rich in good works, generous, and ready to share, thus storing up for themselves the treasure of a good foundation for the future, so that they may take hold of the life that really is life" (1 Tim. 6:17-19).

Which doesn't mean we can ignore in the slightest the reminder in these letters that "he saved us, not because of any works of righteousness that we had done, but according to his mercy . . . so that, having been justified by his grace, we might become heirs according to the hope of eternal life" (Titus 3:5, 7).

That's the core of Paul's personal testimony, that "though I was formerly a blasphemer, a persecutor, and a man of violence . . . I received mercy because I had acted ignorantly in unbelief, and the grace of our Lord overflowed for me with the faith and love that are in Christ Jesus" (1 Tim. 1:13-14).

Both Sides Now

The pastoral letters present both sides of the issue. In an earlier Covenant Bible Study, *Side by Side: Interpreting Dual Stories in the Bible*, I said about scriptures that seem to contradict:

> Does either extreme, faith or works, have much to do with faith in Jesus Christ? I have met Christians who insist that since they "came forward" and expressed their faith in Jesus they can no longer sin. They claim whatever they do is not a sin, whether it's ignoring a parent's medical condition, looking down with contempt on people of other races, or simply living in callous disregard of the sufferings of others around the world, they cannot be touched by reason or argument. They are never wrong.
>
> On the other hand I have met those who are so dedicated to the work of Jesus they'd be hard pressed to quote a single verse of a gospel outside the Sermon on the Mount. Jesus becomes a convenient hat rack on which to hang their arguments.
>
> If there is any conundrum associated with scripture, any apparent contradiction for which we should give thanks, it may be that the tension between faith and works is essential

to building the real body of Christ. Every denomination, every small Bible study group, each racial and ethnic enclave, all the Christians spread across every continent, should be pulling each other back and forth, challenging, teaching, and most of all, loving each other.

Life is messy. It's never fully resolved. Things don't always have to work out. When it comes to the great questions, do we have to have an answer today, or can it wait until next Tuesday? Most of all, can we give ourselves time to work on these problems together? (73)

What are we to make of an apparent contradiction? Perhaps nothing more than this from Paul: "The saying is sure and worthy of full acceptance, that Christ Jesus came into the world to save sinners—of whom I am the foremost" (1 Tim. 1:15).

One More Thing
One aspect of the community of faith not discussed in these letters but present in both the ancient household church and the modern congregation is communion. Perhaps the subject does not make its appearance in these letters because it was no longer a controversy. But it certainly was a reality within the household of God.

All the authors listed in this study's bibliography concur that communion for the first Christians consisted of a full meal and was probably practiced daily. Roman households worked together in crafts, industries, and/or farming, and it was important for the whole family to praise the god of their profession at meal times. Because of this, new believers could no longer participate in family worship or meals. So they formed new families with other Christians, and therefore shared professions, meals, and prayers with other believers.

Without any government safety net, Christians relied on each other for shelter and sustenance. Their communion was spiritual and practical—life giving in both a physical and eternal sense.

Discussion and Action

1. First, articulate what you (or your congregation) stand for. Then reflect honestly about how you or your congregation are known in the community. In what ways do these two perspectives match? In what ways do they differ?

2. When you were a child, what were you told would get you into heaven? What is your opinion now? What, in general, do you think Christians believe is the path to salvation? How do you feel about the "once saved, always saved" position described in this chapter?

3. Think of activities or fundraisers that cost more than they produce. How important is it to participate in activities that make us feel good, as opposed to those that may be somewhat impersonal but more effective?

4. Are you more of a faith or works person? Explain your response. Into which category would most of the Christians you know fall? Which do the most good? Which of today's texts speaks more clearly for you? Why?

5. Recall the things of value you thought about in "Personal Preparation" time. What were some of the things you really had to work for? What was their value to you? Compare that with the value of things that were a freely given gift. Did you prize these unearned gifts? How do you compare these two ways of getting things?

6. What do we do when scriptures appear to contradict? Discuss whether it is important to smooth everything over or if it is okay to live with some ambiguity.

7. In what ways might your group engage in organized good works as individuals and as a faith community? In what ways might you organize for group and individual prayer? What form should your evangelistic witness take? Which of these is most important? What balance should you seek?

7

Stupid Controversies, Unprofitable Contentions

Titus 1:10-16; 3:9-11; 1 Timothy 1:3-7; 4:1-11;
2 Timothy 2:14-18, 22-27; 4:1-5

Personal Preparation

1. Read the passages aloud. What can you deduce about some of the controversies that Paul is speaking against? Which make no sense to you? Check a commentary on the pastoral letters for insight.
2. Identify times of frustration you've experienced with your church and/or your faith. Are you still feeling the same about these things, or have you moved on?
3. What controversies have you experienced in the churches to which you have belonged? Were they serious issues? Frivolous? Unimportant? Vital?
4. How does your congregation handle controversy? How well does your church process it? What are the best ways to deal with sensitive matters? How does the way your congregation deals with these sorts of things affect your view of the church?

Suggestions for Sharing and Prayer

1. Greet one another with words of faith as you arrive. Discuss the events of the past week. Share sentence prayers lifting up the joys and concerns you have experienced.

2. Read today's passages aloud. Discuss some of the questions from "Personal Preparation" in light of the scriptures you have just shared.
3. Spend some time with the case study, "What Would Jesus Do?" (see page 75). Begin by having one person read it aloud from beginning to end. Then take half an hour for discussion, either simulating the council meeting described in the text or taking a step back and imagining what might have happened.
4. Close by praying for churches and believers who are struggling with conflict and controversy. Pray for the light of Christ and for clear guidance in these matters. End with the Lord's Prayer.

Understanding

In 1974 I joined a group of college students performing a play about the founding of the Church of the Brethren, the denomination to which I belong. The Brethren were new to me then. We set out from La Verne in southern California, went north to Modesto in the central valley, and then further north yet to Wenatchee, Washington. We then crossed the country to Roanoke, Virginia for the denomination's Annual Conference. We performed our play in over fifty venues, continuing west through Virginia, West Virginia, Maryland, Pennsylvania, Ohio, Indiana, Illinois, Kansas, Colorado, and eventually all the way through New Mexico back to California.

Although I was impressed by my new church home, I couldn't help but notice that some congregations were in turmoil. For some it was questions about the return of Jesus, which was due to happen any moment—thirty-five years ago. For some there were doctrinal questions. Others had complaints about their pastor. It was the summer of Nixon's resignation, so politics cast a pall over some congregations. But the most intriguing controversy involved two competing vitamin salesmen who were splitting the church over the issue of which product was more Christlike.

What Are We Arguing About?
Over the years I've heard of congregations arguing about how to

keep the children quiet, whether there should be indoor plumbing, why they need a nursery, if there should be a flag in the sanctuary, whether they should sing choruses or hymns, if the choir should wear robes or not, and why should those drones they call pastors get paid at all?

Controversies are only stupid when they're about stuff we don't care about. However, when it is one of our own personal hot-button issues we get hot under the collar, the face gets flushed, the throat gets constricted, and we cease to see straight. Over the years as a pastor I've seen it happen for the strangest things. Of course it's not something strange if I care about it!

It is said that medieval theologians argued over how many angels could dance on the head of a pin. I don't know if that's the Dark Ages equivalent of an urban myth, but I do know that after the Treaty of Westphalia put a temporary end to the wholesale slaughter of Christians by other Christians by establishing three legal state religions in Europe, sermons grew more and more distant from the needs of the people. The late historian Don Durnbaugh described one sermon in which a pastor preached for hours on the subject of which cheese it could have been that the people brought to King David in 2 Samuel 17:29. He eliminated one cheese after another until he settled on cheddar.

Settling Disputes

Those who are engaged in missionary work know that there is not always the same wiggle room for subtle controversies when attempting to get seedling churches to grow. No one seems to have enjoyed a good discussion—or argument— more than the apostle Paul, but in these letters Paul seems quick to dismiss those who disagree with one or two warnings. Maybe he'd had enough, and that's why he counseled Titus to "avoid stupid controversies, genealogies, dissensions, and quarrels about the law, for they are unprofitable and worthless" (Titus 3:9).

Churches that are well settled can handle vigorous discussion—sometimes—but there are places where this is unprofitable. Paul seems concerned that the churches overseen by

Titus may be ill-equipped to sort their way through complex theological and cultural controversies that cast more heat than light.

Some of the controversies involved Christians with a Jewish background who insisted that all ethnic groups adopt their ethnic practices—practices which Paul himself continued to observe throughout his life, but which he did not consider mandatory for all. These are old arguments, already settled by the Council of Jerusalem in AD 49. Paul is against reopening a dead issue.

But if someone quotes the Bible out of context, or strings a series of unconnected verses together into a biblical sampler, then certain unbiblical beliefs or practices can sound sensible. This is a reminder that real Bible study includes setting a passage in the larger context.

Take the "gangrene" spread by Hymenaeus and Philetus, "who have swerved from the truth by claiming that the resurrection has already taken place" (2 Tim. 2:17-18). Hymenaeus had already been named as one who had "suffered shipwreck in the faith" (1 Tim. 1:19-20). I haven't a clue what this supposed controversy might have been about, unless it was simply that the Jesus train had already pulled out of the station and everybody left behind was out of luck. Either way, members of the household had latched on to something they considered biblical and were rocking the boat and "upsetting the faith of some" (2 Tim. 2:18).

But it can be hard to turn off the voices of those who are related to half the church and who have a history with a congregation. Sometimes church members simply accept the fact that certain people are going to make trouble. It's just the way they are, they explain.

One thing I have discovered in my ministry is that there are some who simply like to cause trouble. Can these individuals always be allowed to hold sway? Church growth experts suggest that for some churches to grow they have to shrink a little—those gatekeepers who insist on setting a divisive agenda have to be shown the door. This goes against the grain for those of us who want to include everyone, but Paul is suggesting there are some discussions that are just too toxic.

Deal With It

How do we handle such matters? Churches don't know. Jesus tells us to forgive seven times seventy right after the famous passage in Matthew 18, which is used to justify "the ban" or "avoidance" when handling erring brothers and sisters. Every group has to have some sort of discipline. At some point enough is enough. But how much is enough? And how do we fairly administer discipline within the church when we are all imperfect?

In the midst of all of this, Paul insists that right doctrine and sound teaching must be the foundation of the fellowship. So he writes: "The saying is sure and worthy of full acceptance. For to this end we toil and struggle, because we have our hope set on the living God, who is the Savior of all people, especially of those who believe. These are the things you must insist on and teach" (1 Tim. 4:9-11).

Perhaps the best answer is for small groups to allow everyone to freely interpret scripture while working together to test a hypothesis against the group's knowledge and experience. If we are the household of God then we should work as fellow servants of God, not as rulers who speak unassailable truth from on high. It is not enough, after all, to simply say, "the Bible says it, I believe it, that settles it," if we're not in agreement about what exactly the Bible says.

Accepting checks and balances, as well as the occasional chiding from a group that practices accountability, forbearance, and love, might help us avoid stupid controversies and unprofitable contentions.

Might.

Discussion and Action

1. Talk honestly about whether members of this group feel safe and secure enough to handle all topics, even the most sensitive ones. Is your church a safe place to discuss such things? Why, or why not? What must take place before sensitive topics can be discussed?
2. Should new members of churches get dumped on immediately with all the old arguments that have been brewing

for decades in churches, or is there a time to say enough, we're done? Explain your answer.

3. In Titus 1:12, Paul makes a disparaging remark about Cretans. They were a people proud of their ancient heritage and had fiercely resisted both the Greeks and the Romans before being subsumed into the empire. Their independence may have been mistaken for stubbornness by outsiders. How does it feel to find a racial stereotype in scripture? Was it justified in this case? If so, why? When have you been guilty of making a disparaging remark? When have you been a verbal victim?

4. Talk about whether there are instances when language can be as violent as physical abuse. Give examples that explain your response. How do you rank verbal abuse against other sins? Think about times when you may have victimized other people or groups by your choice of language. How did it feel when you realized you had thoughtlessly or deliberately spread misinformation about people? Discuss how to make amends, if possible, in such situations.

5. Under what circumstances have you heard people you admire make ignorant statements? How do you respond to church people who make false statements? How comfortable are you in challenging people about such remarks? When and where is the best time to do so?

8

The Initiative of God:
Essentials of Faith
Titus 2:11-15; 3:3-7; 1 Timothy 1:12-17;
3:14-16; 4:12-16; 2 Timothy 1:13-14; 2:11-13

Personal Preparation

1. Read the selected passages aloud. Mark those portions you find most interesting. If there are familiar phrases in these passages, take note of them.
2. Make a list of your favorite passages from the Bible. What do they say? What do they say about you?
3. Focus your heart upon those who need prayer this week. Make a list and attempt each day to spend concentrated time in prayer for those people.
4. The Nicene Creed and the Apostles' Creed are printed on pages 76 and 77. If your congregation or denomination has a statement of faith or a creed you recite, bring it to the "Sharing and Prayer" session. If you don't know if such items exist, talk with your pastor or check your denomination's website.

Suggestions for Sharing and Prayer

1. As you gather, share with one another your favorite verses or stories from the Bible. Tell how you first encountered this verse or story, if you remember, and why it is important to you.
2. Read today's passages aloud. Compare them with the creeds printed on pages 76 and 77 or other statements of

faith you might have brought along. Talk about whether you find creeds helpful or limiting in explaining your faith. What "tools" have you found helpful in explaining your faith to others?

3. What would your group include in a statement of faith? Try creating a brief statement of the essentials of faith. After, look together at what you wrote. How did you define yourselves: more by declaring what you are not or more by declaring whose you are?

4. As you consider the shared beliefs of your group and your church, focus also on the issues of health and wholeness. If you are so led, share some of the difficulties or infirmities you are facing. Pray for the well-being of all group members.

5. Some communities of faith use anointing for healing to complement the work of doctors and traditional medicine, recognizing that we are all partners with God in healing. Consider holding an anointing service using the resource printed on page 78.

6. Spend some time singing favorite hymns. Try singing from memory, perhaps one stanza only. Close with "Immortal, Invisible, God Only Wise."

Understanding

According to science fiction writer Arthur C. Clarke, every great idea goes through three stages:

1. It'll never work.
2. It might work, but what good is it?
3. I'm glad I thought of it.

Once the initial skepticism is overcome, it's easy to own an idea or even claim credit for it. But Paul wants us to confess that all our best ideas have their source in God—and maybe to admit as well that we resisted God's great ideas for a good deal longer than necessary.

God has taken the initiative in reaching out to us, instructing us, and sharing his grace with us. These passages speak to the essentials of faith and the saving action of God.

This is the fun stuff. These are some of the inspiring passages that make me want to attribute these letters to Paul, no matter what the experts might say. Getting past the chaff, we finally put our hands on some kernels of truth. In other places the author identifies trouble spots or writes about rules and regulations. In these passages, he inspires.

So in Titus 2:12-13, Paul writes of the need "in the present age to live lives that are self-controlled, upright, and godly, while we wait for the blessed hope and the manifestation of the glory of our great God and Savior, Jesus Christ." This sort of life is necessary because:

> We ourselves were once foolish, disobedient, led astray, slaves to various passions and pleasures, passing our days in malice and envy, despicable, hating one another. But when the goodness and loving kindness of God our Savior appeared, he saved us, not because of any works of righteousness that we had done, but according to his mercy, through the water of rebirth and renewal by the Holy Spirit. This Spirit he poured out on us richly through Jesus Christ our Savior, so that, having been justified by his grace, we might become heirs according to the hope of eternal life (Titus 3:3-7).

These words are important to those of us who are schooled in self-reliance. Independence can be good, but a Christian is called to a life of interdependence upon God and one another.

God Cannot Deny Himself

Titus 2:11-14 is one of the scriptures that congregations following the Revised Common Lectionary readings use on Christmas Day. I remember one year puzzling over the text, unable to figure out how I'd use it. The answer came from an unexpected source. I was teaching my regular weekly Bible study at the local jail, focusing on the Gospel of John as I remember, when one of the prisoners said my words reminded him of this passage from Titus. He opened his Bible to that place and expounded for a couple of minutes. Suddenly I had my Christmas sermon! (Yes, I gave him credit.)

These words from 2 Timothy 2:11-13, which also speak to the initiative of God, inspired me decades ago to write an article called "Brethren Basic": "The saying is sure: If we have died with him, we will also live with him; if we endure, we will also reign with him; if we deny him, he will also deny us; if we are faithless, he remains faithful—for he cannot deny himself."

Back in the ancient early days of home computers, many of us still wrote programs for the primitive machines using computer languages like BASIC. Central to all programming languages is the if-then statement: *if* something takes place, *then* a particular consequence will follow. This passage describes several if-thens that make perfect sense: Act well towards God, and God will act well towards you. Act poorly, and God will turn away from you. But then it throws one in that totally undoes this logic: Despite our faithlessness, God will still respond with faithfulness "for he cannot deny himself" (2:13). This steadfast love of the Lord is a consistent theme that finds expression in Jeremiah and Lamentations, as well as other places in the Old Testament.

Bible 3:16

When I was in seminary, someone reminded me that John 3:16 isn't the only 3:16 that merits attention. Keep in mind this is all coincidence. The first biblical manuscripts were written without any chapter or verse divisions, no spaces between words, and very little punctuation. Verse numbers were added about 500 years ago, or only about a fourth of the shelf life of the Bible. All that aside, 1 Timothy 3:16 is a good example of this happy chance: "Without any doubt, the mystery of our religion is great: He was revealed in flesh, vindicated in spirit, seen by angels, proclaimed among Gentiles, believed in throughout the world, taken up in glory."

This confession of faith practically sings, and some think it may well have been an early church hymn. The doxology, "to the King of the ages, immortal, invisible, the only God, be honor and glory forever and ever" (1 Tim. 1:17), is the inspiration for my favorite hymn, "Immortal, Invisible, God Only Wise."

Paul attempts to give encouragement to his audience by reminding them that he was the first sinner, a persecutor of the faith, but "Christ Jesus came into the world to save sinners—of whom I am the foremost" (1 Tim. 1:15).

It is God who has taken the initiative to establish and maintain a relationship with humanity. God's love has resulted in mercy, even to Paul, who calls himself the worst of sinners, and he uses himself as an example for others. God is reaching out to all of humanity so that all may become heirs of the promise made to Abraham.

These things should be at the heart of preaching (see 1 Tim. 4:12-16), ahead of all the quarreling about the contentious issues or the household codes. Because problems demand attention, much of the content of these three letters has to be directed at those who are part of the trouble. But these passages speak to the need to get past foolish arguments and back to the proclamation of the gospel, the good news of the salvation God offered to all. Free!

This is the message that is spoken through all of scripture. It is the good treasure that is dwelling with us. We are saved by grace, the gift of God.

All of us.

Discussion and Action

1. What is your favorite hymn? What does that hymn say about your faith and practice? Recite a stanza from memory, if you can. What is the place of hymns in the way we express our faith? Then shift to recalling Bible verses you can recite from memory. Why are these verses important to you? Is the ability to recite scripture important to expressing faith? Explain your answer. Which are easier to recall from memory, hymn lyrics or scripture verses? What implications might this have in sharing your faith?

2. Who is the most inspirational speaker you've ever heard? What were the circumstances and when did it take place? What about the message inspired you?

3. Who exactly are we proclaiming? Think back to your discussion during "Sharing and Prayer" time. What does it say about us if we define ourselves by what we are not, rather than by whose we are?

4. Recite aloud the creeds printed on pages 76 and 77. In what settings, if any, does your church use one or both of these? In addition or alternatively, do you have some sort of confession of faith? Does 1 Timothy 3:14-16 work for you, or do you need more? Explain.

5. What does it mean to have acted ignorantly (see 1 Tim. 1:12-18)? What is your view on forbearance for those who have not yet heard the gospel? What limits, if any, are there on God's mercy? On God's patience?

6. From the scriptures you have read and the teaching of the churches you have attended, what is your understanding of God's plan? How does the author's description of God's love in terms of "if-then" statements match or dispute your position on God's plan?

9

All Faith Is Local
Titus 3:12-15; 1 Timothy 1:18-20;
2 Timothy 1:15-18; 4:9-15, 19-22

Personal Preparation

1. Read the passages aloud. Make a drawing that illustrates how you are connected with many people—family members, people at work, church, school, and even people from your past.
2. Have you ever received or given a personal greeting that has made a difference in a church, family, work, or play situation? Reflect on why this particular greeting stands out.
3. Name some unforgettable people who really affected your life, for good or for ill. What made these people unique? Pray over these people or over their memory.
4. Reflect on the importance of greeting people and of knowing something of their history and background. Visualize each group member in turn. Who do you know best? Who do you know least?

Suggestions for Sharing and Prayer

1. Greet each other with the words of 2 Timothy 4:22, "The Lord be with your spirit. Grace be with you."
2. Take time to share what has been going on this past week.
3. Then sit in a circle, making sure all are comfortable. Return to 2 Timothy 4:22, and meditate on it in a *lectio divina* format.

- The group leader reads the verse aloud, inviting members to focus on one word or phrase that seems to jump out at them.
- The leader reads the verse again, and everyone sits in silence for a time, reflecting on their word or phrase and opening their hearts to the Spirit of God.
- After a minute or two, an individual from the group (perhaps someone of the opposite gender from the leader) reads the verse aloud. Again, listen and pray.
- The leader reads the verse aloud for a fourth and final time.
- After a few moments, the leader invites the group to sing a selected hymn.
- Take a little time to share the words or phrases that caught your attention and why.

4. After everyone takes time to stand and stretch, resume the time of "Sharing and Prayer" by inviting people to recall a caring person who told the truth in their lives. Talk about how you responded to this person at the time. What about later? Think about times when a person you respected made a statement founded in ignorance or racism? How did you feel about that? How did you respond?

5. Pray sentence prayers in honor of the difficult truths that need to be told.

Understanding

Living in Los Angeles, it was inevitable that I would meet a few celebrities. When our kids were little we took them to see *A Midsummer Night's Dream*, directed and starring Kenneth Branagh. Afterwards we went backstage, where I spoke with him and got his autograph. Emma Thompson was not yet widely known. While I didn't ask for her autograph, she got down on her hands and knees and spoke with my then three-year-old son Jacob about gardens and fairies. That memory is better than an autograph.

More important than spotting Stevie Wonder and Mel Torme are the real celebrities I've known—high school English teachers, great cooks at churches, extraordinary saints who hold churches together, my aunt who made tamales too hot for just about everyone but we always asked for seconds and thirds.

Everyone knows unforgettable people. Some are famous. Others are known only to a small circle, but their memories inspire tears, laughter, grimaces, sighs, and gentle smiles. Local congregations have their legends.

In the ancient world, personal letters were public documents used as vehicles for sending greetings, and Paul's pastoral letters are no exception. In writing to Timothy and Titus, Paul says "hey" to some pretty big names, a veritable *Who's Who* of first-century Christianity and a reminder about the diversity in background and practice in the early church.

For Example . . .

Priscilla and Aquila are one of the most mobile and active couples engaged in New Testament ministry. Priscilla (sometimes referred to as Prisca) is usually mentioned first. In our own experience, this usually signifies that the wife is the leader in many things, especially in the couple's public persona. In this case, it is also possible that she had a higher social status.

The two were tentmakers, like Paul, so they had a lot in common. It is likely that as they moved around they set up a household in which they practiced their craft to pay the bills.

Priscilla and Aquila were later exiled from Rome because of the trouble messianic Jews caused there. Their expulsion in AD 51 is mentioned by the Roman historian Suetonius, as well as the book of Acts. The two then traveled to the Greek city of Corinth, where they provided hospitality to Paul. They accompanied Paul to Ephesus, where they met and instructed Apollos, and eventually worked their way back to Rome. When Paul's letter to that city arrived, he praised them not only as co-workers but as two "who risked their necks for my life" (Rom. 16:4). It seems likely that they hosted house churches in Rome, Corinth, Ephesus, and later in Rome again.

Tychicus is also an intriguing figure. He is mentioned in Acts, Ephesians, and Colossians, along with 2 Timothy and Titus. A native of Asia Minor, he is described as "a dear brother and a faithful minister in the Lord" (Eph. 6:21). His name means "lucky." That looks like a slave name to me, yet Paul describes him as a close associate and trusted emissary. In contrast to the class-conscious Roman society and despite instructions to slaves to be obedient, perhaps we see here how the transformed household of God overshadowed the importance of appearing normal to Roman society.

Apollos was an influential teacher from Alexandria in Egypt, a center of great learning. Acts describes him as "an eloquent man, well-versed in the scriptures" (Acts 18:24). Alexandrian Jews were known for their allegorical interpretations of scripture. Interestingly, although the book states that though he "taught accurately the things concerning Jesus . . . he knew only the baptism of John" (Acts 18:25).

When Priscilla and Aquila heard Apollos preach incorrectly, they did not call him out in public, but met with him privately to fill in the gaps in his knowledge. This not only demonstrates that kindness rather than competition motivated the founders of the faith, but also that despite what Paul seems to say elsewhere, women did teach men. This is consistent with what some suggest would have been the case in house churches, where typically women managed day-to-day affairs. The fact that it was not public instruction makes this more likely.

Luke the physician wrote the two-volume work known as the Gospel of Luke and the Acts of the Apostles. That makes him the author of a substantial portion of the New Testament. He endeavored to demonstrate to a Roman patron that while the gospel is turning the world upside down, it is not intrinsically treasonous. Utilizing the tools of rhetoric, he demonstrated that the different way of living espoused by Jesus and his followers changed the world without touching the political structure. His is the most elegant Greek in the New Testament.

Luke is not only a historian, but a participant. The word "we" is used in four different sections of Acts (16:10-17; 20:5-

15; 21:7-18, and 27:1–28:16), clearly indicating that he traveled with Paul. In letters written to Colossae and to Philemon, he is identified as one of those who stayed with Paul in prison.

Mark, author of the earliest gospel, is the originator of a whole new genre. He may well have been present at the arrest of Jesus if he is, as some suspect, the young man who escaped from the garden of Gethsemane by running away from his clothes when they were seized by the arresting guards. His mother Mary, who owned the upper room, was herself a major figure in early Christian history. Her house, which seems later to have served as a house church, was the home to the Last Supper, important resurrection appearances, the descent of the Spirit at Pentecost, and was such a natural sanctuary for intercessory prayer that Peter knew to show up there after he was freed from prison by an angel.

Mark traveled with Barnabas and Paul on their first great missionary journey but left for reasons unknown before their travels were complete. This led to a breakup with Paul (see Acts 15:36-41), but later references in Colossians 4:10 and Philemon 24 make it clear that there was an eventual reconciliation These passages also demonstrate that like Luke, Mark stayed with Paul in prison. Paul begs Timothy to bring Mark back to him because he is so useful.

Our knowledge of the achievements of many of these people makes those about whom we know little or nothing all the more intriguing: Zenas the lawyer, Artemas, Crescens (from Galatia, where the Celts healed Paul's eyesight), Erastus, Trophimus, Eubulus, Pudens, Linus, Claudia, Carpus. This last person is the one caring for Paul's coat—how Paul must have shivered in prison.

Special praise comes to Onesiphorus and his household, because he sought Paul out in prison in Rome. Not all did so.

Paul also mentions enemies: "By rejecting conscience, certain persons have suffered shipwreck in the faith; among them are Hymenaeus and Alexander, whom I have turned over to Satan, so that they may learn not to blaspheme" (1 Tim. 1:19-20). Is this Alexander the coppersmith mentioned in 2 Timothy 4:14?

What's What

So what's the point? The point is that these passages are ground-
ed in local congregations. It's all personal. All faith is local.
There is nothing theoretical about the local congregation. Every
small group, fellowship, house church, meetinghouse, little
brown church in the vale, and cathedral comes with the baggage
of history. There are heroes and, yes, probably a villain or two
in every congregation.

In thanking and praising those who have stood by him in
bad times as well as good, and by calling to mind those who
have impeded the gospel, Paul reminds us that what happens at
the local level matters. Earth-shaking, eternity-shattering events
are occurring, and we're either standing in the way or furthering
the gospel of Jesus Christ.

You could be in somebody's letter. That's a pretty sobering
thought.

Discussion and Action

1. Reflect on individuals who have influenced your life for
    good or ill. Are these people "famous" in the local con-
    gregation or in family life? Name and pray about some
    of the unforgettable people from your congregation.
    Make these come alive for each other through stories,
    memories, and songs.

2. How important is it that we explain details so others will
    know those who we are talking about? How do you
    respond when someone in your congregation assumes
    everyone knows past history, when, of course, new
    members know nothing of those who are being spoken
    about?

3. Congregations in Paul's day typically consisted of a
    series of house churches that shared a larger identity but
    met in small groups. How are small groups linked in
    your congregation? In general, are people's faith identi-
    ty tied more to the congregation or to their small group?

4. Chart your church, showing the relationships between
    small groups, large groups, and the denomination. What
    are the connections forwards and backwards, up and

down? What do these connections reveal about the organizational system?

5. Which character mentioned by Paul do you find the most interesting or attractive? If there are individuals in your life who remind you of biblical characters, name them and tell why.

6. As a group, make a list of believers beyond your church to whom you ought to send greetings. Take time now to write notes or assign people the tasks of sending greetings and offering words of encouragement before the next group session.

7. The story of Mark and Paul is one of alienation and reconciliation. If you have experienced one or both in your life or in your church, tell the stories. Discuss whether it is possible for Christians to get along all the time. What causes such difficulties, in your opinion?

10

All Will Be Well, and Farewell!
1 Timothy 6:6-16; 2 Timothy 1:8-10;
3:1-9; 4:6-8, 16-18

Personal Preparation

1. As in past sessions, read the scriptures for this session out loud. What difference, if any, has it made to read aloud rather than silently?
2. Look over the "Famous Last Words" printed on pages 79-80. What other famous last words do you remember? If you can, write down last words from individuals who were important in your life. What would you like your own last words to be?
3. In the first session you reflected on your initial impressions of these letters. Now that you have studied them, compare your former attitude with your current thinking. Bring both reflections to the group session.
4. Reflect on the "Seven Last Words of Jesus" as recorded in the Gospels (see page 80). Pray and meditate over each verse.

Suggestions for Sharing and Prayer

1. Greet one another as you arrive. Share joys and concerns from the past week. As you gather in a circle, lift up sentence prayers on behalf of one another.
2. Read the session's scriptures out loud, as per the pattern you have adopted during these sessions. Take time to react to the passages. Discuss the difference it has made to read passages aloud rather than silently.

3. In "Personal Preparation" time for the first session you were asked to write a short paragraph about your initial reflections on these letters. Read these paragraphs out loud, along with the ones you wrote for today. Compare and contrast your varying conclusions. Why do you think people experience the same document in similar and different ways? What do you think informed your hearing? What has changed in your perception of these three letters?

4. Read aloud the selected "Famous Last Words" on pages 79-80. Add other famous last words you can recall to the list, along with last words from people you have known. Then share what you'd like for your own last words, which you were invited to compose during "Personal Preparation" time. Conclude by reading aloud the "Seven Last Words of Jesus" on page 80. What, if any, similarities do you find in the last words from historical figures, people you've known, your own, and those of Jesus? What differences do you find?

5. Pray the "Seven Last Words of Jesus" as a group. One person begins by saying the first verse, then another person says the second verse, and so on through all seven. Pause between verses for silent reflection and prayer.

6. Close by singing "Guide My Feet" and "In the Bulb There Is a Flower."

Understanding

I was present when Dora Hershberger passed away. She was lying in a hospital bed, seemingly unconscious, with her family gathered around her. They were speaking to her, though they were not certain if she could hear. Her granddaughter rushed from college, arriving after a three-hour drive.

At some level Dora must have known what was said, because she clung to life until her granddaughter arrived. Moments later every line on the monitors leveled out and Dora passed away. Tears fell all around, but there was also the sense that this was a good death.

One definition of a *good* death is passing away peacefully at a ripe old age, surrounded by family, in possession of one's faculties, having accomplished most of life's goals. Sadly, this is not always possible.

According to historian Drew Gilpin Faust, good death in the nineteenth century meant dying at home, sharing words of comfort with the family who surrounded you, giving advice, telling the truth, and professing your faith as you passed away. In *This Republic of Suffering: Death and the American Civil War*, Faust recounts how this became nearly impossible for thousands dying on battlefields far from home.

People struggled to find substitutes for an experience they considered crucial. Comrades wrote to assure relatives that their loved one had experienced a good death. Sergeant Amos Humiston from New York died at Gettysburg gazing at a photograph of his children since he couldn't die in their midst. And some soldiers, mortally wounded, wrote blood-stained letters to assure their families that they had died well.

Passages from 1 and 2 Timothy can be taken as the apostle Paul's last words. He shares advice with those who matter to him, and assures them that as a prisoner facing execution he will die well because he has lived well and accomplished all he might expect in this life.

The athletic imagery here is consistent with Paul's other writings. He compares his life to a race finally finished. He also speaks of being poured out as a drink offering, very similar to the image of the death of Jesus in Philippians 2. Death is interpreted as triumph.

Even so, Paul seems alone and abandoned. Unlike the house arrest described in the final chapter of Acts, which most likely ended in the dismissal of charges, Paul now paints a picture of harsh imprisonment, abandonment, and loneliness. This caused him to reflect on the end of life and the beginning of hope. He looks not only to his own reward, but to the glory that will be shared by all.

Paul seems to call to mind the words of Jesus from the cross asking forgiveness for his executioners, when he writes, "At my first defense no one came to my support, but all deserted me. May it not be counted against them!" (2 Tim. 4:16).

We Are the Champions

This last testament is paired with words of victory. Even some who question whether Paul wrote these letters admit there is a great likelihood that these words are authentic: "I have fought the good fight, I have finished the race, I have kept the faith. From now on there is reserved for me the crown of righteousness, which the Lord, the righteous judge, will give me on that day, and not only to me but also to all who have longed for his appearing" (4:6-8).

The point is that just as athletes train for a purpose, so each person can anticipate the crown Paul believes he will soon be wearing. That's the point of all this training in life. Death waits for us all. Sooner or later we all have to make our peace with that fact.

Christian writer C. S. Lewis recalled a conversation with a young woman on a train. The subject of death came up, but the woman shrugged it off. She expected that by the time she was old, science would have eliminated death altogether. While few people would hold that opinion today, it seems as if sometimes death catches people by surprise. In addition to the natural grief and shock we all feel, there can be outrage and shock that it could happen at all.

One sees this especially in the untimely and usually tragic death of a young person. The sorrow is understandable, and yet it seems never to have occurred to some that driving wildly on icy roads, or indulging in dangerous narcotics, or engaging in dangerous behavior might have a fatal consequence.

On the other hand, one sees children's books, movies, and television shows that confront the inevitability of death and the importance of celebrating life. Certainly it is important to be prepared for the fact it must happen.

We All Get a Turn

One thing that makes for a good death is the feeling that life has been well-lived and major goals have been accomplished. And yet no one accomplishes everything. J. R. R. Tolkien struggled for years to complete his massive novel, *The Lord of the Rings*, and on more than one occasion he despaired that he would finish it or that his life's work would amount to anything. Then he awoke one morning with an idea for a story. Uncharacteristically for someone who was used to worrying every word of every page to death, he quickly wrote a short story titled *Leaf by Niggle.*

In the story, a painter named Niggle knows he must make a journey at some time in the future, but he puts off preparing for it while he attempts to finish a canvas depicting every detail of a great tree. The demands of caring for his neighbor prevent Niggle from finishing when despite his protests he must make the journey, which is a symbol for his death. Eventually, all that remains of his unfinished work is a single leaf displayed in a museum, but in the meantime Niggle's spiritual journey renders any fears about a worldly legacy moot. It's a tender and beautiful story, and according to his biographers, writing the story freed Tolkien to finish his life's work.

Alexander Mack, Jr. (1712-1803) was an important figure in Colonial America, serving as spiritual leader of the German-speaking separatists known as Dunkers, or the Brethren, for more than fifty years. Not long before his death at age 92, he wrote some last words to his Germantown congregation. He did not choose to sum up his life or give spiritual advice. Rather, he took his fellow believers to task for not taking care of a widow who needed their aid.

Identifying himself as "an aged stranger and pilgrim on this earth," Mack admitted that the woman was very difficult and unstable, and though they could not readmit her to the flock, they could care for her. Too weak to visit them personally, he wrote, "I could not assume then that I would live to see New Year's Day, about four months hence. I did, however, have every right to assume that when the mortal shell of mine is buried, the New Testament is not buried with it. And it is there that the Lord speaks and says: 'It is more blessed to give than to receive!'" (Durnbaugh 230).

Perhaps this study—and these biblical letters—will have done their work if we look beyond ourselves to the shared ministry of the household of God, an eternal work which finds us all together in the divine endeavor. If we have run the good race, fought the good fight, and finished the course, we will indeed receive, with everyone else, the crown of righteousness the Lord has prepared for us upon that day.

Discussion and Action

1. In addition to his final testimony, the apostle Paul gives a series of warnings as well as some advice. Share these verses in your own words. What is the theme or purpose of these words? What would your own words of advice be?

2. To the extent that you are able, describe your best and worst encounters with death. How would you describe a *good* death? How does our culture view death? If any in the group have lived for a time in another culture, share what you know about death in those places. Do you think these cultural views are generally realistic and healthy, or are they unhealthy? Why?

3. What are the expectations for funerals in your community? Talk about what you usually experience at visitations and funerals at your church or in the surrounding area. What are the origins of these customs?

4. Reflect on all ten sessions in this study. Now that you have heard these letters, in whole or in part, two or three times, what seems important to you? To what extent do you think your opinion of these passages depends on your place in life? What words are important to you? Which are not? Why?

5. What is your view of the ancient church, the apostle Paul, and Christian history now that you have shared time together with these sessions? In what ways has your viewpoint changed? In what ways has your viewpoint remained the same?

6. What theme or issue impressed you in your hearing and study of these letters? What parts of the content seemed antiquated or outdated?

7. Paul gives Timothy some last advice about churches. Why do you think these items were so important to him? If any of these concerns sound familiar, name them. End your study with prayer for God's wisdom and discernment as you seek to be faithful members of the household of God.

Resource Pages

Chapter 6

Trial: Faith vs. Works—Biblical Simulation
You are part of the Council of Jerusalem in AD 49. The apostle Paul has arrived to meet with James, the brother of Jesus, and other apostles. James comes with believers from both Jewish and Gentile backgrounds. They are among the Jerusalem Christians who are distressed that Paul baptizes people and establishes churches without requiring they practice Jewish religious and ethnic customs.

Here is the timeline for this simulation:
   Preparation—15 minutes
   Simulation—15 minutes
   Debriefing—10 minutes

Preparation
Divide into two groups of about equal size. One group is aligned with James and the other group is aligned with Paul. The study leader will serve as moderator.

For both groups:
   • Select a leader who speaks, not exclusively, for the group.
   • Select a scribe who takes notes.
   • Read assigned scriptures. You may not get to all of them. Remember, virtually none of the New Testament writings would have been written by AD 49. These are intended to help establish positions or attitudes.
   • Discuss scriptures and the points you hope to make in the meeting.

James and the Jerusalem Group
   Scriptures:
   • Jeremiah 7:23
   • Genesis 15:1-6

Paul and the Empire Group
   Scriptures:
   • Jeremiah 31:31-34
   • Genesis 15:1-6

- James 2:14-24
- James 1:27
- 1 Timothy 1:8-11; 6:17-21
- Philippians 2:1-11
  (Jesus was obedient)
- Matthew 5:1-16

Sample talking points:
- Jeremiah says obey God's
  command
- Stand up for the faith as
  once given
- Make clear Abraham saved
  by works
- All become part of covenant
  body through obedience

- Galatians 3:1-14
- Romans 4:1-25
- Titus 3:3-8
- Philippians 2:1-11
  (All come to Jesus)
- Joel 2:28-32

Sample talking points:
- Jeremiah says God
  does something new
- Stand up for the
  New Covenant
- Make clear Abraham saved
  by faith
- Gentiles are part of the
  covenant body through
  faith

Simulation
Meet as equals in a circle. The two leaders will be invited by the study leader to make one-minute statements on their position regarding believers being baptized without requirement to obey Jewish biblical law.

Each group leader may respond to the other leader's statement. Groups may consult privately before responding. Keep discussion on a calm, biblical basis.

Debriefing
At the end of fifteen minutes, define areas of agreement and disagreement. Discuss how the simulation felt. If there is time, consult Acts 15:1-29 and Galatians 2:1-10 for two accounts of what occurred.

Chapter 7

What Would Jesus Do?—Case Study
There are times when controversies arise in churches around divisive issues that can split churches or ruin reputations. Those who raise these questions may use scripture to lend legitimacy to their causes.

For instance, in Matthew 22:15-22 the Pharisees attempt to trap Jesus between the religious fervor and the nationalism of the people by asking if it was proper to pay taxes to the emperor. If he said yes, then he would be a collaborator. If he said no, he would be a traitor.

And in Matthew 22:23-33 the Sadducees, who did not believe in the resurrection of the dead, attempted to dismiss the belief in a confrontation with Jesus by reducing the matter to an absurdity. The Levirate law of Deuteronomy 25:5 required a man to marry his brother's widow for the purpose of supplying heirs to preserve the family's title to land. The Sadducees told a story about a woman who had seven brothers die on her in turn; they asked Jesus whose wife she would be in the resurrection.

In both cases, Jesus refused to answer the question on their terms. He relied instead on common sense and scripture.

In the following case study, a mythical church is presented with a religious controversy. Employing both common sense and your knowledge of scripture, as well as today's scripture passages, use the case study as the basis for discussion of how to handle tough issues.

Naaman's Faith
David Divider and Mary Misinformed are two recent members of the congregation. They are popular, active, and have brought in a number of new members. Thanks to them, worship is more vibrant and there is a feeling that things are happening.

Recently, however, a controversy has developed. David and Mary have insisted that 2 Kings 5:1-14 makes it clear that believers who are sick should act in faith, and like Naaman, be immersed seven times in flowing water in order to be healed.

They insist that if one truly has faith they will take no vitamins, medicines, herbals, nor should they visit doctors and follow their advice.

Some believe them, and have joined them in abstaining from traditional medicine. Others are wary, but afraid of offending them. The pastor seems confused about what to do.

David and Mary have begun to accost new members to convince them to follow their advice. The church has called a council meeting to discuss the matter.

Read today's scriptures, as well as the other passages mentioned in this case study. Consider the following questions.

- What is your view of the matter?
- Must the church be united on this issue? If so, why?
- Does the church need to take official action? If so, why?
- What is the best way to deal with this matter?
- Should church officials on the regional or denominational level be asked to join the discussion? If so, who and when?
- What sorts of scriptures can you marshal on your behalf?
- What does common sense tell you?

Chapter 8

The Nicene Creed

We believe in one God,
    the Father, the Almighty,
    maker of heaven and earth,
    of all that is, seen and unseen.
We believe in one Lord, Jesus Christ,
    the only Son of God,
    eternally begotten of the Father,
    God from God, Light from Light,
    true God from true God,
    begotten, not made,
    of one Being with the Father;
    through him all things were made.
    For us and for our salvation
    he came down from heaven,
    was incarnate of the Holy Spirit and the Virgin Mary

and became truly human.
For our sake he was crucified under Pontius Pilate;
he suffered death and was buried.
On the third day he rose again
in accordance with the Scriptures;
he ascended into heaven,
and is seated at the right hand of the Father.
He will come again in glory to judge the living and the dead,
and his kingdom will have no end.
We believe in the Holy Spirit, the Lord, the giver of life,
who proceeds from the Father and the Son,
who with the Father and the Son is worshipped
and glorified,
who has spoken through the prophets.
We believe in one holy catholic and apostolic Church.
We acknowledge one baptism for the forgiveness of sins.
We look for the resurrection of the dead,
and the life of the world to come. Amen.

The Apostles' Creed

I believe in God, the Father almighty,
creator of heaven and earth.
I believe in Jesus Christ, God's only Son, our Lord,
who was conceived by the Holy Spirit,
born of the Virgin Mary,
suffered under Pontius Pilate,
was crucified, died, and was buried;
he descended to the dead.
On the third day he rose again;
he ascended into heaven,
he is seated at the right hand of the Father,
and he will come to judge the living and the dead.
I believe in the Holy Spirit,
the holy catholic Church,
the communion of saints,
the forgiveness of sins,
the resurrection of the body,
and the life everlasting. Amen.

A Basic Service of Anointing
Read aloud Lamentations 3:19-24 and/or James 5:13-16:

> The thought of my affliction and my homelessness is worm-
> wood and gall! My soul continually thinks of it and is
> bowed down within me. But this I call to mind, and there-
> fore I have hope: The steadfast love of the LORD never ceas-
> es, his mercies never come to an end; they are new every
> morning; great is your faithfulness. "The LORD is my por-
> tion," says my soul, "therefore I will hope in him." (Lam.
> 3:19-24)

> Are any among you suffering? They should pray. Are any
> cheerful? They should sing songs of praise. Are any among
> you sick? They should call for the elders of the church and
> have them pray over them, anointing them with oil in the
> name of the Lord. The prayer of faith will save the sick, and
> the Lord will raise them up; and anyone who has committed
> sins will be forgiven. Therefore confess your sins to one
> another, and pray for one another, so that you may be
> healed. The prayer of the righteous is powerful and effec-
> tive. (James 5:13-16)

Then say:

> We are gathered together to anoint our (brother/sister) in the
> presence of God for (give reason for anointing). We come
> boldly forward with courage, because Jesus commanded us
> to pray "Give us this day our daily bread." We come meek-
> ly with the fears of Jesus when he prayed, "Not my will, but
> thine." Knowing that in the midst of a broken world God
> wills wholeness in body, mind, and spirit, I now anoint you
> with oil (the leader anoints the forehead with oil in the shape
> of three crosses) for the forgiveness of your sins, the grant-

ing of peace to your soul, and the restoration of wholeness to your body.

The leader then lays hands, one on top of the other, on the head of the one being anointed. Others present may lay their hands upon the leader's hands, or upon a shoulder, until all are touching. After the leader prays, a silence follows in which others may pray aloud or silently as they choose. The leader closes with a brief spoken prayer, followed by the Lord's Prayer in which all may join.

For additional resources and information on anointing, see pages 253-268 in *For All Who Minister* (Brethren Press, 1993) or your denomination's minister's manual.

Chapter 10

Famous Last Words
Daniel Webster: "I still live."

Thomas Jefferson and John Adams, political rivals as well as sometime partners, both died on July 4, 1826, the fiftieth anniversary of Independence Day. Jefferson's last words were, "This is the Fourth?" Adams is reported to have said, "Thomas Jefferson still survives."

General John Sedwick (1813-1864), fighting for the Union side at the Battle of the Wilderness: "They couldn't hit an elephant at this dist—."

Ethan Allen, in 1789, after his doctor told him, "Sir, I fear the angels are waiting upon you," responded by saying, "Waiting, are they? Waiting are they? Well, let 'em wait."

Douglas Fairbanks: "Never felt better."

Thomas de Mahay, Marquis de Favras (1744-1790), was caught by the radicals of the French Revolution as he plotted to help

Louis XVI escape. Convicted of treason after a two-month trial, he was handed his official death sentence by the court clerk as he was led to the scaffold. His last words were, "I see that you have made three spelling mistakes."

Edmund Gwenn (1875-1959), best known for playing the role of Santa Claus in *Miracle on 34th Street* (for which he received an Oscar), was asked on his deathbed if dying was difficult. He replied, "Dying is easy. Comedy is difficult."

Conrad N. Hilton (1887-1979), hotel magnate, was asked on his deathbed for his last words of wisdom for the world: "Leave the shower curtain on the inside of the tub."

The Seven Last Words of Jesus
"Eli, Eli, lema sabachthani?" that is, "My God, my God, why have you forsaken me?" (Matt. 27:46)

"Father, forgive them; for they do not know what they are doing." (Luke 23:34)

"Truly I tell you, today you will be with me in Paradise." (Luke 23:43)

"Father, into your hands I commend my spirit." (Luke 23:46)

"Woman, here is your son . . . Here is your mother." (John 19:26-27)

"I am thirsty." (John 19:28)

"It is finished." (John 19:30)

Bibliography

Durnbaugh, Donald F., ed. *Brethren in Colonial America.* Elgin, Illinois: Brethren Press, 1967.

Faust, Drew Gilpin. *This Republic of Suffering: Death and the American Civil War.* New York: Alfred A. Knopf, 2008.

Finger, Reta Halteman. *Of Widows and Meals: Communal Meals in the Book of Acts.* Grand Rapids: Eerdmans, 2007.

Milavec, Aaron. *The Didache: Faith, Hope, & Life of the Earliest Christian Communities, 50-70 C.E.* New York: The Newman Press, 2003.

Osiek, Carolyn, and Margaret Y. MacDonald with Janet H. Tulloch. *A Woman's Place: House Churches in Earliest Christianity.* Minneapolis: Fortress Press, 2005.

Sanger, S. F. and D. Hayes. *The Olive Branch.* Elgin, Illinois: Brethren Publishing House, 1907. Reprinted 1997.

Williams, Ritva H. *Stewards, Prophets, Keepers of the Word: Leadership in the Early Church.* Peabody, Mass.: Hendrickson Publishers, 2006.

Other Covenant Bible Studies

1 Corinthians: The Community Struggles . . . . .Inhauser
Abundant Living: Wellness from a
    Biblical Perspective . . . . .Rosenberger
Biblical Imagery for God . . . . .Bucher
Country Seer, City Prophet . . . . .Neff/Ramirez
Covenant People . . . . .Heckman/Gibble
Daniel . . . . .Ramirez
Ephesians: Reconciled in Christ . . . . .Ritchey Martin
Esther . . . . .Roop
The Exile . . . . .Kline
Exodus: Freed for the Journey with God . . . . .Burkholder
Five Festal Scrolls . . . . .Neff/Ramirez
The Gospel of Mark . . . . .Ramirez
Hebrews: Beyond Christianity 101 . . . . .Poling
Hymns and Songs of the Bible . . . . .Parrott
In the Beginning . . . . .Kuroiwa
James: Faith in Action . . . . .Young
Jeremiah . . . . .Kinzie
Jonah: God's Global Reach . . . . .Bowser
The Life of David . . . . .Fourman
The Lord's Prayer . . . . .Rosenberger
Love and Justice . . . . .O'Diam
Many Cultures, One in Christ . . . . .Garber, ed.
Mystery and Glory in John's Gospel . . . . .Fry
Parables of Matthew . . . . .Davis
Paul's Prison Letters . . . . .Bynum
Presence and Power . . . . .Dell
The Prophecy of Amos and Hosea . . . . .Bucher
Psalms . . . . .J. D. Bowman
Real Families: From Patriarchs to Prime Time . . . . . .Dubble
Revelation: Hope for the World in Troubled Times . . .Lowery
Romans: Church at the Crossroads . . . . .Wiles
Sermon on the Mount . . . . .R. Bowman
Side by Side: Interpreting Dual Stories in the Bible . . .Ramirez
Spirituality of Compassion: Studies in Luke . . . .Finney/Martin
Uncovering Racism . . . . .Reid/Reid

Voices in the Book of Job ....Neff
When God Calls ....Jessup
Wisdom ....C. Bowman

Each book is $7.95 plus shipping and handling. For a full description of each title, ask for a free catalog of these and other Brethren Press titles. Major credit cards accepted. Prices subject to change. Regular Customer Service hours are Monday through Friday, 8:30 a.m. to 5:30 p.m. CST.

Brethren Press • 1451 Dundee Avenue • Elgin, Illinois 60120
Phone: 800-441-3712 • Fax: 800-667-8188
E-mail: brethrenpress_gb@brethren.org
www.brethrenpress.com